The Adventures
of
Tom Sawyer

The Adventures of Tom Sawyer

Mark Twain

Adapted by
WILLIAM KOTTMEYER

Phoenix Learning Resources
New York & St. Louis

The Phoenix Everyreaders

The EVERYREADERS were selected from the great literature of the world and adapted to the needs of today's students. This series retains the flavor of the originals, providing mature content and dramatic plot structure, along with eye appeal designed to motivate reading.

This approach was first developed in the renowned St. Louis Reading clinic by Dr. Kottmeyer and is the direct outgrowth of wide and successful teaching of remedial reading.

A high interest level plus the carefully controlled vocabulary and sentence structure enable pupils to read the stories easily, confidently, and with enjoyment.

ISBN 0-7915-1376-9

1 2 3 4 5 6 7 8 9 0 99 98 97 96 95 94 93

CONTENTS

Chapter 1

"Tom!"

No answer.

"Tom!"

No answer.

"Where is that boy? You, TOM!"

The old lady pulled her glasses down. She looked over them around the room. Then she pulled them up and looked under them. She never looked *through* them for the boy. These glasses were her fancy pair. They were not made to see through. She was very, very proud of them. She frowned.

"Well, if I ever get hold of you, I'll..." poking under the bed with a broom. No boy under the bed! Only the cat.

"I never did see the beat of that boy!"

She went to the open door. She looked at the tomato vines in her little garden. No Tom there either. She raised her voice.

"Yoo hoo! Tom!"

There was a little noise behind her. She turned. She made a lucky grab and caught a small boy by the seat of his pants.

"There!" she cried. "I should have remembered that closet. What have you been doing in there, you rascal?"

"Nothing, Aunt Polly."

"Nothing? Look at your hands! And look at your mouth! What *is* that stuff?"

"I don't know, Aunt Polly."

"Well, I know. It's jam. That's what it is. I've told you forty times to leave that jam alone or I'll skin you. Hand me that switch."

"Look behind you, Aunt Polly."

The old lady whirled around. She snatched her skirts aside. That quick the boy was gone. Out the door he flew, and over the high board fence he went.

Aunt Polly looked surprised a moment. Then she laughed.

"Darn that boy!" she said. "I never learn. He's played me tricks enough like that. But old fools is the biggest fools there is. Can't learn an old dog new tricks, as they say. He knows just how long he can pester me till I get my dander up. I ain't doing my duty by that boy. Spare the rod and spoil the child, they say. But he is my own dead sister's boy, poor thing. I ain't got the heart to whip him. Every time I do hit him, my old heart almost breaks. It's hard to make him work Saturdays. All the other boys are off and can play."

Tom played hookey that day and he had a very good time. He got back home just in time to help Jim, the little colored boy. They had to saw the next day's wood and split kindling. As they worked, Tom told Jim about his adventures. Of course, Jim did most of the work. Tom's younger brother Sid had done his share by picking up the wood chips.

Aunt Polly was pretty sure Tom had been playing hookey again. She thought she was pretty good at catching Tom telling lies.

"Tom," she said at supper, "it was hot in school, wasn't it?"

"Yes, ma'am."

"Awful warm?"

"Yes, ma'am."

"Didn't you want to go swimming, Tom?"

"No, ma'am. Well, not very much."

The old lady reached out her hand and felt Tom's shirt. Tom left his shirt on when he swam. The shirt was dry, though. Tom saw the way the wind was blowing.

"Some of us pumped water on our heads," he said. "Mine's still damp. See?"

Aunt Polly knew Tom had beat her to that one. Tom's shirt collar was not part of his shirt. It had to be sewed on. When he went swimming he did take his collar off.

"Tom," she said. "you didn't have to undo your shirt collar where I sewed it on, did you? When you pumped the water, I mean. Open your jacket."

Tom opened his coat. The shirt collar was sewed tight to his shirt.

"I see," said Aunt Polly. "I was sure you'd played hookey and went swimming. I was wrong, I see."

"Say, Aunt Polly," said Sid, "I thought you sewed his collar on with white thread. It's sewed on with black now."

"Why, I did sew it on with white. Tom!"

But Tom didn't wait. Out the door he went.

"Sid, I'm going to give you a licking for that!" he yelled.

In a safe place Tom pulled out two needles he kept stuck in his coat collar. One needle had white thread. The other one had black.

"She'd never have seen that," said Tom. "That sneaky Sid had to tell. Sometimes she uses black, sometimes white. I wish she'd stick to one or the other. But I'm going to beat Sid up for telling."

The summer days were long. It was not dark

4

yet. Tom, out walking, ran into a stranger. The boy was a little bigger than Tom. He was well dressed. He had shoes on—and it was only Friday. He even wore a tie. He looked like a city boy. Tom didn't like city boys. Neither boy spoke. When one moved, the other moved. They kept face to face. At last Tom spoke.

"I can lick you!" he said.

"I'd like to see you try it."

"Well, I can do it."

"No, you can't."

"Yes, I can."

"No, you can't."

"Can!"

"Can't!"

"What's your name?"

"None of your business."

"I'll *make* it my business."

"Well, why don't you?"

"If you say much, I will."

"Much! Much! Much! There now."

"You think you're smart, don't now? I could lick you with one hand tied behind me."

"Well, why don't you do it?

"Look at that silly hat."

"You can lump that hat if you don't like it. I dare you to knock it off."

"I ain't afraid to."

"Yes, you are."

Tom made a line in the dirt with his big toe.

"I dare you to step over that line. I'll lick you so you can't stand up."

The new boy stepped over the line.

"Now you said you'd do it. Let's see you do it."

"Don't crowd me now. You better look out."

"Why don't you do it?"

"For two cents I will do it."

The new boy took two pennies out of his pocket. He held them out and laughed. Tom slapped them to the ground. In a flash both boys were rolling in the dirt. They pulled and tore at each other's hair and clothes. They punched and scratched and kicked. They covered themselves with dirt—and glory. Soon Tom was sitting on top of the new boy, pounding him with his fists.

"Holler enough" he yelled.

No answer. The new boy tried to get free. He was crying—mainly from anger.

"Holler 'nuff!" The pounding went on.

At last the stranger cried, "Nuff!" Tom let him up.

"Now," said Tom, "that'll learn you. Better look out who you're fooling with next time."

The new boy went off brushing the dirt from his clothes. He was still sobbing. He yelled at Tom and told him what he'd do to him next time. As soon as Tom turned his back, the new boy snatched up a stone. He threw it. It hit Tom between the shoulders. The boy turned then and ran like a deer. Tom chased him all the way home. He stood at the gate, daring the boy to come back out. The boy just made faces at him through the window. At last the boy's mother came out. She called Tom a bad, nasty brat and told him to go home.

Tom got home pretty late that night. He crawled through his bedroom window. There sat Aunt Polly, waiting for him. When she saw his dusty, torn clothes, she lost her temper.

"There'll be no playing for you tomorrow!" she said. "You're going to work all day Saturday."

Chapter 2

Saturday morning came, bright and fresh and clear. Tom came out on the sidewalk. He carried a bucket of whitewash and a long-handled brush. He looked at the fence. All gladness left him. Thirty yards of board fence nine feet high! Groaning, he dipped his brush and passed it along the top plank. He did it again. He looked at the little whitewashed streak. Then he looked at all the unwhitewashed space. He sat down sadly. Jim came skipping out the gate with a tin pail. Tom had always hated bringing water from the town pump. Now it did not seem bad at all. There were always boys and girls there. They would just sit or trade playthings while waiting their turns. The pump was only a hundred and fifty yards away. Jim never got back with a bucket of water in under an hour. Even then somebody had to go after him.

"Say, Jim, I'll fetch the water if you'll whitewash some."

Jim shook his head.

"Can't, Mars Tom. Old Aunt Polly told me to go get this water. She said not to fool around with anybody. She said Mars Tom goin' to ask me to whitewash some. Said I should tend to my own business."

"Oh, never you mind what she said, Jim. That's the way she always talks. Give me the bucket. I won't be gone only a minute. She won't ever know."

"Oh, I dasn't, Mars Tom. Aunt Polly'd tear my head off. Yes she would."

"*She!* She never licks anybody. Whacks 'em over the head with her thimble. Who cares for that? She talks awful, but talk don't hurt. I'll give you a marble. I'll give you a white one."

Jim was tempted. Tom held it in his hand.

"It's a bully taw, Jim."

"Say," said Jim, "that is a nice one! But Mars Tom, I'm afraid—"

"If you will, I'll show you my sore toe."

That was too much for Jim. He put down the pail and took the marble. He bent over Tom's foot as he unwound the bandage. A minute later he was flying down the street. He had his bucket back and his rear end was burning. Tom was whitewashing as hard as he could. Aunt Polly was going back with a slipper in her hand.

Tom's hard work didn't last very long. He began to think of the fun he had planned. Soon the boys would come by to play. They'd make fun of him for having to work. He got out what he had in his pockets. There were bits of toys, marbles, and trash. He might trade some of the junk off for work, but he didn't have much. He gave up the plan of trying to buy the boys. At that dark moment he thought of a great idea.

He picked up his brush and went to work. Pretty soon Ben Rogers came by. He was eating an apple and pretending to be a steamboat. He was the boat, the captain, and the bell, all together.

"Stop her, sir," he cried. "Ting-a-ling-ling! Ding-dong-ding! Chow-wow! Chow-wow!" He swung his arm round and round as if he were the big paddle wheel on a steamboat.

Tom went on whitewashing. He didn't even

look up at Ben. Ben stopped and stared at him.

"Oh, oh! Poor Tom! Got to work, don't you?"

No answer. Tom stepped back like an artist looking at his painting. Then he gave the brush another easy sweep. He stepped back again to see how it looked. Tom's mouth watered for the apple, but he stuck to his work.

"Hello, old chap. You got to work, hey?"

Tom turned suddenly, as if he was surprised.

"Why, it's you, Ben! I didn't see you."

"Say—I'm going swimming, I am. Don't you wish you could? But of course you'd rather work, wouldn't you? Course you would."

Tom looked at Ben, sort of surprised.

"What do you call work?" he said.

"Why, ain't that work?"

"Well, maybe it is and maybe it ain't. All I know is it suits Tom Sawyer."

"Oh come now. You don't mean to let on that you like it?"

Tom's brush kept on moving.

"Like it? Well, I don't know why I shouldn't like it. Does a boy get a chance to whitewash a fence every day?"

Ben hadn't thought of that. Ben stopped eating his apple. Tom added a touch or two like an artist would. Ben watched every move.

"Say, Tom, let *me* whitewash a little."

Tom thought about it. He almost gave Ben the brush. Then he changed his mind.

"No, no, it wouldn't do, Ben. You see, Aunt Polly's awful picky about this fence. It's right here on the street. If it was the back fence, I wouldn't mind. *She* wouldn't mind. This fence has got to be done very careful. There ain't one boy in a thousand—maybe two thousand—that can do it the way it should be done."

"Oh, is that so? Oh, come now. Let me just try. Only just a little. I'd let you, if you was me, Tom."

"Ben, I'd like to, honest Injun. But Aunt Polly—well, Jim wanted to do it. She wouldn't let him. Sid wanted to do it. She wouldn't let Sid. Don't you see how I'm fixed? If you was to mess it up—"

"Oh, shucks. I'll be just as careful. Now let me try. I'll give you a bite of my apple."

"Well, here—no, Ben. Now don't. I'm afraid."

"I'll give you *all* of the apple, Tom."

Tom gave up the brush. While Ben worked and sweated in the sun, Tom sat on a barrel. He stood in the shade. Tom ate his apple. Boys came by every little while. They came to make fun of Tom, and stayed to whitewash. When Ben tired out, Tom had traded the next chance to Billy Fisher for a kite. When he tired out Johnny Miller bought in for a dead rat and a string to swing it with. On and on it went, hour after hour. When the middle of the afternoon came, Tom was rich. He had twelve marbles, a mouth harp, a spool cannon, a key. He had a tin soldier, two tadpoles, six firecrackers. He had a kitten with one eye, a brass door knob, a dog collar, and a window sash.

He had a nice, lazy time with plenty of company. The fence had three coats of whitewash. If he hadn't run out of whitewash, he'd have cleaned out every boy in town.

Tom had learned a great lesson: To make somebody want something, make it hard to get. Work is what you *have* to do. Play is what you don't *have* to do.

Tom went inside to report to Aunt Polly.

Chapter 3

Aunt Polly was sitting by an open window. She was nodding over her knitting, almost asleep. Her glasses were propped up on her gray head. She was sure Tom must have run off long ago. And so she was surprised when he came in.

"May I go out and play now, Aunt Polly?"

"What? Already? How much have you done?"

"It's all done, Aunt Polly."

"Tom, don't lie to me. I can't bear it."

"I ain't. It *is* all done."

Aunt Polly went out to see for herself. She would have been glad to see a fifth of the fence done. She found the whole fence whitewashed. It was not only coated. It was coated and recoated and recoated! There was even a white streak added to the ground. She was so surprised she could hardly speak.

"Well, I never! There's no getting around it. You can work when you want to, Tom. Well, go on and play. Come back sometime this week or I'll tan you!"

She was so overcome by his work, she wanted to reward him. She took him into the closet and gave him a big red apple. On the way out he swiped a doughnut.

Then he skipped out. He saw Sid on the outside stairway to the second floor. Clods of dirt were lying around. In a minute the air was full of flying clods. Tom threw one after another at Sid. Three or four hit him. Before Aunt Polly could stop it, six or seven had landed. Tom was over the fence and gone. He felt better for having gotten even with Sid for telling about the black thread.

Later that afternoon Tom was on the way home. He passed by the house where Jeff Thatcher lived. There was a new girl out in the garden. She was a lovely little girl with yellow hair braided in two long tails. She wore a pretty white dress. Tom fell in love at first sight. Amy Lawrence, his girl friend, faded out of his mind. He had thought he loved Amy. It had taken him months to win her. When she had said she liked him too, he'd been the proudest boy in the world. That was just seven days ago. Now, in one moment, it was all over.

When the girl looked his way, Tom started to show off. But before long the girl was on her way into the house. Tom came up to the fence and leaned on it. She stopped a moment on the steps. She turned and tossed a pansy over the fence to him. Then she was gone. Tom picked the flower up and slipped it inside his jacket. He hung around the fence till it got dark. All through supper he had a dreamy look on his face. He took a good scolding for throwing the clods. He tried to steal sugar under his aunt's nose and got his knuckles rapped.

"Aunt, you don't whack Sid when he takes it."

"Well, Sid don't pester a body the way you do, Tom. You'd always be in that sugar if I didn't watch you."

Soon she stepped into the kitchen. Sid reached for the sugar bowl. He wanted to show Tom that *he* could get away with it. But Sid's fingers slipped. The bowl dropped and broke. Tom was so glad *he* hadn't done it that he said nothing. He planned just to sit still and let her ask who had done it. Aunt Polly came back in. When she saw the broken bowl, she lost her temper. The next moment Tom went sprawling on the floor! Aunt Polly raised her hand to swat him again.

"Hold on now!" he yelled. "What are you belting me for? Sid broke it!"

Tom wanted to hear her say she was sorry.

"Well," she said, "I guess you've been into some other things I never found out about."

She *did* feel bad. She wanted to give Tom a few kind words, but she just couldn't admit she'd been wrong. Tom knew she was sorry, but that didn't help. He went out to walk by himself. He went past Jeff Thatcher's house again, hoping to see the new girl. A candle was lighting up the shade on a second story window. He climbed the fence and made his way through the plants. He stood there a long time, staring at the window. At last he lay down on the ground under it. Suddenly the window flew up.

"Get out of there!" yelled a voice. A bucket of water followed, soaking poor Tom from head to foot.

He jumped up. Something came flying out of the window, nearly hitting him. Over the fence went Tom.

When Tom got home and undressed for bed, he hung up his wet clothes. Sid, who slept with him, saw them. He didn't say anything, but made up his mind to tell Aunt Polly in the morning. Tom jumped into bed and didn't say his prayers at all that night.

"I'll tell Aunt Polly about that, too," said Sid to himself. "She'll tan him good."

Chapter 4

Sunday breakfast was over. Aunt Polly had family prayers and Bible reading. Tom got to work learning his Bible verses for Sunday school. Sid had learned his days ago. Tom had to learn five verses this morning. He found the shortest ones he could. At the end of half an hour, he hadn't learned them at all. Tom's mind was on other things. Mary took his book to hear him recite.

"Blessed are the—a—a—"

"Poor—"

"Oh, yes—poor. Blessed are the poor—a—a"

"In spirit—"

"In spirit. Blessed are the poor in spirit, for they—"

"Theirs—"

"For theirs. Blessed are the poor in spirit, for theirs is the kingdom of—of— Why don't you tell me, Mary? What do you want to be so mean for?"

"Oh, Tom, you poor thick-headed thing, I'm not teasing you. I wouldn't do that. You must go and learn it again. If you do, I'll give you something nice. There, now. That's a good boy."

"All right! What is it, Mary? Tell me what it is."

"Never you mind, Tom. You know if I say it's nice, it *is* nice."

"You bet that's so, Mary. All right. I'll go at it again."

Tom did. And he learned them. Mary gave him a brand new Barlow knife worth fifteen cents.

Mary gave him a tin basin of water and some

soap. He went outside the door. There he set the basin on a little bench. He dipped the soap in the water and laid it down. He rolled up his sleeves. Then he poured the water gently over the ground. He went into the kitchen. He wiped his face on the towel behind the door. But Mary took the towel away.

"Now ain't you ashamed, Tom! You mustn't be so bad. Water won't hurt you."

Mary filled the basin again. This time he took a deep breath and began. He came back in the kitchen with both eyes shut. The suds and water were dripping from his face. His face was clean, but his neck was filthy. Mary took over. When she got through he looked a lot better. His hair was neatly brushed. Mary got out his Sunday suit. She buttoned his coat and turned his big white collar down over his shoulders. Then she brushed him off and put his straw hat on. He hoped Mary would forget his shoes. She didn't. She coated them with tallow as people did in those days. He put them on, but he hated them. Mary was soon ready. The three set out for Sunday school. Tom hated it. Sid and Mary loved it.

Sunday school hours were from nine to half past ten. After that the three went to church. At the door Tom stopped.

"Say, Billy, have you got a yellow ticket?"

"Yes."

"What will you take for it?"

"What will you give?"

"Piece of candy and a fishhook."

"Let's see 'em."

Tom showed. The trade was made. Then Tom traded two marbles for three red tickets. Then he got a few blue ones. He met other boys as they came in. He went on buying tickets of different colors for fifteen minutes longer. He went in, then, and sat with his class. The first thing they did was to recite Bible verses. Nobody knew his verses perfectly, but they all stumbled through with a little help. Then each one got his reward in small blue tickets. Each one had a Bible verse on it. You got a blue ticket for every two verses you learned. Ten blue tickets equaled a red one. Ten red tickets equaled a yellow one. For ten yellow tickets you got a Bible—worth about forty cents in those days. You had to learn two thousand verses, then, to get a Bible. That often took two years! And yet Mary had won two Bibles this way. A boy with German parents had won four or five! He once recited three thousand verses without stopping. The strain was too great, though. He was little better than an idiot from that day on. That was a sad day for the Sunday school. They always "showed off," as Tom said, by having him come up for another Bible.

Only the older pupils were able to keep their tickets and stick to it long enough to get a Bible. And so, giving out one of these prizes was a big deal. Tom had never really wanted a Bible, but he longed for the glory that came with it.

The Sunday school superintendent was a skinny fellow named Walters. He was about thirty-five. He had a sandy beard and sandy hair. Sooner or later he would stand in front and make his Sunday speech. It went about like this:

"Now, children, I want you all to sit up as straight and pretty as you can. I want you all to listen a minute or two. There! That's it! That is the way good little boys and girls should do. I see one little girl who is looking out the window. I am afraid she thinks I am out there. Perhaps she thinks I am making a speech to the little birds out there. I want to tell you how good it makes me feel to see your bright clean little faces. You are here learning to do right and be good."

Some whispering had been going on during Mr. Walters' speech. It had started when some visitors came in. Lawyer Thatcher had come in with a very old man. With them were a fine looking, middle-aged gentleman and his wife. The lady had a child by the hand. It was the pretty little girl who had tossed Tom the flower! Tom's heart turned over.

The visitors were seated in front of the church. As soon as Mr. Walters finished his speech, he introduced the visitors to the Sunday school. The middle-aged man turned out to be the county judge. Everybody stared at the great man. This was the famous Judge Thatcher, brother of their own town lawyer. Jeff Thatcher now came forward.

"Look at him, Jim," whispered a boy. "He's going up there! He's going to shake hands with him. Don't you wish you was Jeff?"

As the lessons went on, Mr. Walters walked around proudly. Everybody showed off for the visitors. There was only one thing wanting to make Mr. Walters happy. That was a chance to hand out a Bible and show off the pupil who had learned two thousand verses. A few pupils had a few yellow tickets, but none had enough. Mr. Walters had been asking the star pupils about the tickets. He would have given his right arm to have that German boy back with a sound mind.

And now, at this moment, when hope was dead, Tom Sawyer came forward. He had nine yellow tickets, nine red tickets and ten blue ones.

"May I have my Bible?" he said.

This was a thunderbolt out of a clear sky!

Walters wouldn't have expected Tom Sawyer to learn two thousand Bible verses in the next ten years. But there was no getting around it. The tickets were there. They sat Tom up next to the judge. Mr. Walters announced to the Sunday school that Thomas Sawyer would be given a Bible. The boys were green with envy. But those who suffered most were the ones who had traded him tickets.

Mr. Walters handed Tom the Bible with as much joy as he could manage. He knew, of course, that something was wrong here. He would have been surprised if Tom could have recited five or ten verses.

Amy Lawrence was proud and glad. She tried to catch Tom's eye, but he wouldn't look her way. Tom had to shake hands with the judge. He could hardly speak. This was *her* father! The judge put his hand on Tom's head. He called him a fine little man. He asked what his name was. The boy stammered and choked, but he got it out at last.

"Tom."

"Oh, no. It's not Tom. It's—?"

"Thomas."

"Ah, that's it. I thought there was more to it. But you have another one, I dare say. You'll tell it to me, won't you?"

"Tell the gentleman your other name, Thomas," said Mr. Walters. "And say *sir*. You mustn't forget your manners."

"Thomas Sawyer, sir."

"That's it! That's a good boy. Fine boy. Fine, manly little fellow. Two thousand verses is a very, very great many. You'll be a great man and a good man some day, Thomas. Then you'll look back and say, 'It's all because of Sunday school. It's due to good Mr. Walters, who gave me a beautiful Bible.' That is what you will say, Thomas. And now tell me and this nice lady some things you've learned. We're proud of little boys who learn. No doubt you know the names of all twelve of Jesus' followers. Won't you tell us the names of the first two?"

Tom was looking sheepish. He blushed. His eyes fell. Mr. Walters' heart sank. He was sure Tom couldn't answer *any* questions.

"Answer the gentleman, Thomas. Don't be afraid."

Tom still said nothing.

"Now I know you'll tell *me,*" said the lady. "The names of the first two were—"

"David and Goliath?" said Tom.

Chapter 5

Monday mornings made Tom Sawyer very unhappy. Monday meant school, and Tom did not like school. Tom lay in bed thinking. He wished he was sick. If he were sick, he could stay home from school. Was anything wrong? Could his stomach be upset? For a while he thought that might be true. But no, that wasn't going to work. He found that one of his upper front teeth was loose. He was starting to groan when he remembered that Aunt Polly would pull it out. That would hurt. He remembered once hearing a doctor talk about a boy's sore finger. Something happened and the boy almost lost the finger. Tom couldn't remember the name of the thing that had made the finger worse. Now Tom already had a sore toe. Couldn't the same thing happen to *his* toe? Tom pulled up his sore toe from under the sheet. Maybe it was worth trying. He started to groan.

Sid slept on.

Tom groaned louder. He thought he could feel some pain in the toe now.

Sid kept on sleeping. Tom took a rest. Then he groaned louder.

Sid snored on.

"Sid! Sid!" yelled Tom. He shook him. That worked, so Tom began groaning again. Sid stared at him.

"Tom! Say, Tom!" he cried.

But Tom did not answer.

"What's the matter, Tom?" He shook Tom and

looked at him closely.

"Oh, don't shake me, Sid!"

"What's the matter, Tom? I must call Aunt Polly!"

"No, never mind. It might be over by and by. Don't call anybody."

"But I must! *Don't* groan so, Tom. It's awful. How long have you been this way?"

"Hours. Ouch! Don't move, Sid. You'll kill me."

"Tom, why didn't you wake me sooner? Tom, don't! It makes my flesh crawl to hear you! What *is* the matter?"

"I forgive you everything, Sid. Everything you've ever done to me. When I'm gone—"

"Oh, Tom, you ain't dying, are you? Maybe—"

"I forgive everybody, Sid. Tell 'em so. And Sid, you give my window sash and my kitten with one eye to that new girl in town. Tell her—"

But Sid had grabbed his clothes and was gone. Tom groaned louder.

Sid flew downstairs.

"Oh, Aunt Polly," he cried. "Tom's dying!"

"Dying?"

"Yes, ma'am. Don't wait! Come quick!"

"Bunk! I don't believe it!"

But she went upstairs with Sid and Mary at her heels. Her face *did* get white.

"You, Tom! Tom, what's the matter with you?"

"Oh, Aunt Polly, I'm—"

"What's the matter with you, child?"

"Oh, Aunt Polly, my sore toe is *mortified!* "

The old lady sank down into a chair and laughed. Then she cried a little. Then she did both together.

"Tom," she said, "to be *mortified* means to be ashamed. You meant to say *putrefied.* That means rotted. Your toe ain't rotted. It ain't

21

ashamed, either, is it? Maybe it should be. What a scare you did give me! Now shut up that nonsense and get out of bed!"

Tom stopped groaning and his toe stopped hurting. He felt a little foolish.

"Aunt Polly, it *seemed* mortified. It hurt so bad I didn't mind my tooth at all."

"Your tooth? What's the matter with your tooth?"

"One of them's loose. It hurts awful."

"There, there, now. Don't start that groaning again. Open your mouth. Well, your tooth *is* loose. That won't kill you. Mary, get me a silk thread. Bring me a chunk of fire out of the kitchen, too."

"Oh, please, Aunt Polly! Don't pull it out! It don't hurt anymore. Please don't. I don't want to stay home from school."

"Oh you don't, don't you? So all this was because you thought you'd get to stay home from school and go fishing? Tom, Tom, I love you so. You try every way you can to break my old heart."

The old lady tied one end of the silk thread to Tom's tooth. She tied the other end to the bedpost. Then she grabbed the hunk of fire. She poked it suddenly almost into the boy's face. He jerked his head back. Now the tooth hung from the bedpost.

As Tom went to school after breakfast, he filled all the boys with envy. The gap in his front upper teeth made him able to spit in a new way. The boys all gathered around him to watch him spit. Another boy had been showing off his sore finger. Now everybody watched Tom. The boy said he didn't think it was so great to spit like Tom. But another boy just laughed and said, "Sour grapes."

Chapter 6

That morning Tom ran into the one boy *nobody* was allowed to play with. That boy was Huckleberry Finn. Huck was the son of the town drunk. All the mothers in town hated and dreaded the sight of him. The boys all liked him and wished they could be free, like him. Tom, too, was under strict orders not to play with him. Of course he did play with him whenever he got a chance. Huck was always dressed in old, castoff clothes. Whenever he wore a coat, it hung almost to his heels. The seat of his pants was baggy. His pants' legs dragged in the dirt.

Huck came and went as he pleased. In fine weather he slept on doorsteps. When it rained or snowed, he slept in empty barrels. He never went to school or to church. He could go fishing and swimming when he pleased. Nobody told him not to fight. He could stay up as late as he pleased. He was always the first boy to go barefoot in spring and the last to put on shoes in the fall. He never had to wash. He never had to put on clean clothes. He could and did cuss and swear. Every boy in St. Petersburg envied him.

"Hello, Huckleberry!" said Tom.

"Hello yourself and see how you like it."

"What's that you got?"

"Dead cat."

"Let me see him, Huck. My, he's pretty stiff. Where'd you get him?"

"Bought him off a boy."

"What did you give?"

"I give a blue ticket and a pig bladder."

"Where'd you get the blue ticket?"

"Bought it off Ben Rogers two weeks ago for a hoop stick."

"Say, what is dead cats good for, Huck?"

"Good for? Cure warts with."

"No! Is that so? I know something that's better."

"I bet you don't. What is it?"

"Why, spunk water."

"Spunk water! I wouldn't give a darn for spunk water."

"You wouldn't? Did you ever try it?"

"No, I ain't. But Bob Tanner did."

"Who told you?"

"Why, he told Jeff Thatcher, and Jeff told Johnny Baker. Johnny told Jim Hollis. Jim told Ben Rogers. Ben told a colored kid and he told me. There now!"

"Well, what of it? They'll all lie. All but the colored kid. Now you tell me how Bob Tanner done it, Huck."

"Why he dipped his hand in a rotten stump where the rain water was."

"In the daytime?"

"Sure."

"With his face to the stump?"

"Yes. I reckon so."

"Did he *say* anything?"

"I don't reckon he did. I don't know."

"Aha! Talk about trying to cure warts with spunk water such a blame fool way as that. Why that ain't going to do any good. You got to go all by yourself to the middle of the woods. Just as it's midnight you back up against the stump. You jam your hand in. You say:

'Barley corn, barley corn, Injun meal shorts

Spunk water, spunk water, swaller these warts.'
Then you walk away quick, eleven steps, with your eyes shut. Then you turn around three times and walk home. You can't speak to anybody. If you speak, the charm's busted."

"Well, that sounds like a good way. That ain't the way Bob Tanner done."

"No, sir, you can bet he didn't. He's the wartiest boy in town. He wouldn't have a wart on him if he'd knowed how to work spunk water. I've took off thousands of warts off my hands that way, Huck. I play with frogs so much that I've always got warts. Sometimes I take 'em off with a bean."

"Yes. A bean's good. I've done that."

"Have you? What's your way?"

"You split the bean. Then you cut the wart to get some blood. You put the blood on a piece of the bean. You dig a hole and bury it about midnight at crossroads in the dark of the moon. Then you burn up the rest of the bean. The piece that's got blood on it will keep drawing. It tries to fetch the other piece to it. That helps the blood to draw the wart. Pretty soon, off she comes."

"Yes, that's it, Huck. But when you're burying it you should say:

'Down bean, off wart,

come no more to bother me.'
That's the way Joe Harper does. But say, how do you cure 'em with dead cats?"

"Why, you take your cat to a graveyard. You go about midnight when a bad guy has been buried. At midnight a devil will come, or maybe two or three. You can't *see* them. Maybe you can hear them talk. When they're taking that feller away, you throw your cat after them. You say, 'Devil follow dead man. Cat follow devil. Warts follow cat.' That will fetch *any* wart."

"Sounds right. Did you ever try it, Huck?"

"No, but old Mother Hopkins told me."

"Well, I reckon it's so, then. They say she's a witch."

"Why, Tom, I know she is. She witched Pap. He came along one day. He sees her witching him. He threw a rock at her. If she hadn't dodged, he'd a got her. Well, that very night he rolled off a shed where he was laying drunk. He broke his arm."

"Say, Huck, when you going to try the cat?"

"Tonight. I reckon they'll come after old Hoss Williams tonight."

"But they buried him Saturday. Didn't they get him Saturday night?"

"Why, how you talk! How could their charms work till midnight? Then it's Sunday. Devils don't mess around much of a Sunday."

"I never thought of that. That's so. Let me go with you?"

"Of course—if you ain't afraid."

"Afraid? It ain't likely. Will you meow?"

"Yes. You meow back if you get a chance. Last time you kept me meowing till old Hays throwed rocks at me. He said, 'Darn that cat!' Well, see you tonight, Tom."

Chapter 7

"Right, Huck. See you tonight."

When Tom reached the little frame schoolhouse, he walked fast. He hung his hat on a peg. He slid into his seat. The teacher was dozing in his chair in front of the room. Tom woke him up.

"Thomas Sawyer!"

"Sir?"

"Come up here. Now, sir, why are you late again?"

Tom was about to lie. But then he saw two long pigtails of yellow hair. It was the new girl! And next to her was the *only empty seat* on the girls' side of the schoolroom.

"I stopped to talk to Huckleberry Finn."

The teacher stared. The pupils wondered if Tom had lost his mind.

"You did what?"

"Stopped to talk to Huckleberry Finn."

"Thomas Sawyer, this is awful! How could you do such a thing? Take off that jacket."

The teacher's arm worked on poor Tom's back till he ran out of switches.

"Now, sir, go and sit with the girls! And let this be a warning to you."

Tom had known that would happen. He sat down on the end of the pine bench. The girl tossed her head and moved a few inches away. By and by the other pupils went back to their books. Tom started to glance at the girl. She turned away. When she looked back, a peach lay in front of her.

She pushed it away. Tom gently put it back. She pushed it away again. Tom pushed it back. This time she let it stay. Tom wrote on his· slate: "Please take it. I got more." He started to draw something on the slate, hiding it with his left hand. By and by the girl tried to see what he was drawing. Tom kept on drawing. At last she spoke.

"Let me see it."

Tom uncovered a house with smoke coming out of the chimney.

"It's nice. Make a man."

Tom drew a man in the front yard.

"It's nice. Now make me coming along."

Tom did so.

"It's ever so nice. I wish I could draw."

"It's easy," said Tom. "I'll learn you."

"Oh, will you? When?"

"At noon. Do you go home to dinner?"

"I'll stay if you will."

"Good! What's your name?"

"Becky Thatcher. What's yours? Oh, I know. It's Thomas Sawyer."

"That's the name they lick me by. I'm Tom when I'm good. You call me Tom, will you?"

"Yes."

Now Tom started to write on the slate. He hid the words from Becky.

"Let me see."

"Oh, it ain't anything."

"Yes it is."

"No, it ain't. You don't want to see."

"Yes, I do. Please let me."

"You'll tell."

"No, I won't."

"You won't ever tell *anybody?*"

"No, I won't."

She put her hand on his. Tom let his hand slip till the words could be seen: "I love you."

"Oh, you bad thing!" She slapped his hand, but she looked pleased.

Just then Tom felt a grip closing on his ear. The teacher raised him from his seat. Tom was marched across the room to his own seat. The whole room giggled. Tom's ear tingled, but he was a happy boy.

When school broke up at noon, Tom whispered in Becky's ear.

"Put on your bonnet. Let on like you're going home. Give the rest of them the slip. Turn down the lane and come back. I'll meet you here."

In a little while the two met at the end of the lane. They had the schoolroom to themselves. They sat together with a slate before them. Tom gave Becky the pencil. He held her hand in his, guiding it, to draw pictures. By and by they just talked.

"Say, Becky, was you ever engaged?"

"What's that?"

"Why, engaged to be married."

"No."

"Would you like to?"

"I reckon so. I don't know. What is it like?"

"Why, it ain't like anything. You tell a boy you won't ever have anybody but him. Then you kiss. That's all. Anybody can do it."

"Kiss? What do you kiss for?"

"Why, that is to—. Well, they always do that."

"Everybody?"

"Why, yes. Everybody that's in love with each other. Do you remember what I wrote on the slate?"

"Y—Yes."

"What was it?"

"I won't tell you."

"Shall I tell you?"

"Y—Yes, but some other time."

"No, now."

"No, not now. Tomorrow."

"Now! Please, Becky. I'll whisper it."

Becky didn't answer. Tom put his arm around her waist. He whispered it ever so softly, his mouth close to her ear.

"Now you whisper it to me—just the same."

"You turn your face away so you can't see," she said. "Then I will. But you must not ever tell anybody. You won't, will you?"

"No, indeed I won't. Now, Becky."

She turned his face away. She bent and whispered, "I—love—you!"

Then she jumped up and ran around the desks and benches. Tom ran after her. At last she was cornered. She held her little white apron over her face.

"Now, Becky, it's all over but the kiss. Don't you be afraid of that. It ain't anything at all. Please, Becky."

By and by she gave up. She let her hands drop. Tom kissed her red lips.

"Now it's all done, Becky. You ain't to love anybody but me. You ain't to marry anybody but me. Will you?"

"No, I'll never love anybody but you, Tom. I'll never marry anybody but you. And you ain't to marry anybody but me, either."

"Of course. That's part of it. And going to school, or going home, you're to walk with me. You choose me and I choose you at parties. That's the way you do when you're engaged."

"It's so nice. I never heard of it before."

"Oh, it's fun! Why, me and Amy Lawrence—"

Becky's big eyes told Tom that he had put his foot in his mouth.

"Oh, Tom! Then I ain't the first one you've been engaged to!" She started to cry.

"Oh, don't cry, Becky. I don't care for her any more."

"Yes, you do, Tom. You know you do."

Tom tried to put his arm around her neck. She pushed him away. He tried again. She pushed him away again. His pride was hurt now. He got up and went outside. He stood there a while, looking at the door. He hoped she would come out and find him. She did not. He went back in at last. She was standing back in a corner, still crying.

"Becky," he said, "I don't care for anybody but you."

No answer. Now she was sobbing hard.

"Becky, won't you say something?"

More sobs.

Tom got out his best prize—a shiny brass door knob. He held it so she could see it.

"Please, Becky, won't you take it?"

She clapped it to the floor. Tom marched out of the school. He never came back at all that day. Becky, too, felt sorry now. She ran to the door. He wasn't there.

"Tom!" she cried. "Come back, Tom!"

No answer. She sat down to cry some more. But now the other boys and girls began to come back. She picked up the brass knob. She wiped her tears away so nobody would see she had been crying.

Chapter 8

At half past nine that night, Tom and Sid were sent to bed. They said their prayers and Sid was soon asleep. Tom lay awake and waited for Huck's meow. He thought it must be morning, but he heard the clock strike only ten. He heard Aunt Polly snore in the next room. A cricket started to chirp. A dog howled. The clock struck eleven. Tom did not hear it. He had dozed off. Suddenly a cat started to howl. A neighbor's window slammed open. An empty bottle crashed against his aunt's woodshed. Somebody cried, "Scat, cat!" Tom was wide awake now. A minute later he was dressed. Out the window he went. He "meowed" once or twice. Then he jumped to the roof of the woodshed. Huck Finn was there with his dead cat. A half hour later they were wading through the tall grass of the graveyard.

The graveyard was on a hill, about a mile and a half out of town. Grass and weeds grew all over. The wind moaned through the trees. The boys talked very little. They found the new grave. They hid behind three big elm trees a few feet from the grave.

They waited a long time.

"Huck, do you think the dead people like for us to be here?"

"I wish I knowed," said Huck. "It's awful spooky here, ain't it?"

Soon Tom grabbed Huck's arm.

"Sh!"

33

"What is it, Tom?"

"Sh! There it is again. Didn't you hear it?"

"Lord, Tom, they're coming! The devils are coming for sure! What will we do?"

"I don't know. Think they'll see us?"

"Oh, Tom, they can see in the dark. I wish I hadn't come."

"Don't be scared. Maybe they won't bother us. We ain't doing any harm. Keep still. Maybe they won't see us."

A sound of voices floated up from the far end of the graveyard. Somebody swinging a lantern came closer.

"It's the devils, sure enough," whispered Huck. "Three of 'em! Lord, Tom, we're goners! Can you pray?"

"I'll try. But don't be scared. They ain't goin' to hurt us. Now I lay me down to sleep. I—"

"Sh!"

"What is it, Huck?"

"They're *people*. One of them is, at least. One of them's old Muff Potter's voice. He's drunk, as he always is—old soak!"

"Say, Huck! I know another voice. It's Injun Joe's voice!"

"That's so! That bloody killer! I'd rather see devils than him. What can they be up to?"

The three men had reached the grave. They stood a few feet from the boys' hiding place.

"Here it is," said the third voice. It was young Dr. Robinson!

Potter and Injun Joe were pushing a wheelbarrow. A rope and some spades lay on it. Muff and Joe started to dig at the grave. They soon had the dirt flying.

"What do they want, Tom?" whispered Huck.

"Why dig up a dead body?"

"Dr. Robinson must want it, Huck. Doctors cut up bodies. They learn how we are put together that way."

Dr. Robinson set the lantern at the head of the grave. He sat down with his back against one of the elm trees. He was so close the boys could have touched him.

"Hurry, men!" he said in a low voice. "The moon might come out soon."

The men growled and kept on digging. At last a spade struck the coffin. In another minute or two the men had hoisted it out on the ground. They pried the lid off with a spade. They got the body out and dumped it on the ground. They got the barrow ready. The laid the body on it and covered it with a blanket.

"Now the cursed thing's ready, Sawbones. You're going to fork over another five or here she stays," said Muff Potter.

"That's the way to talk!" said Injun Joe.

"Look here," said the doctor. "What does this mean? You wanted to be paid before the job was done. Well, I paid you."

"Yes, and you done more than that," said Injun Joe. "Five years ago you drove me away from your father's kitchen one night. I'd come to ask for something to eat. You said I wasn't there for no good. I swore I'd get even with you if it took a hundred years. Your father had me jailed as a bum. Did you think I'd forget? The Injun blood ain't in me for nothing. Now I've *got* you and you're going to pay up."

He had his fist in the doctor's face. The doctor swung suddenly at him and knocked him to the ground. Potter dropped his knife.

"Here, now," he cried. "Don't you hit my partner!"

The next minute he jumped the doctor. The two went at it, trampling the grass and tearing up the ground. Injun Joe sprang to his feet. He snatched up Potter's knife. Then, creeping like a cat, he waited for a good chance. All at once the doctor threw Potter off. He grabbed the heavy board on Williams' grave and clouted Potter to the ground with it. The Indian saw his chance. He drove the knife to the hilt in the young man's chest. The doctor reeled and fell on top of Potter. Blood spurted all over Muff Potter. Tom and Huck sped away in the dark.

Injun Joe stared at the two bodies. Then he stooped and robbed the doctor's body. He put the knife in Potter's open right hand. He sat down on the coffin. Five minutes passed. Potter started to stir and moan. His hand closed on the knife. He raised it, looked at it, and let it fall. He shivered. He looked up at Joe.

"What's happened, Joe?"

"It's a nasty business," said Joe. "Why did you do it?"

"I? I never done it!"

"That kind of talk won't help you, Muff."

Potter grew white.

"I thought I'd got sober. I'm all mixed up. Can't remember anything. Tell me, Joe. Honest, now old fellow, did I do it? Joe, I never meant to."

"Why, you two was fighting. He belted you one with the board. You fell flat. Then up you come. You grabbed the knife and jammed it into him. As he fell, he hit you one last time. Your lights went out. Here you laid till just now."

"I didn't know what I was doing. I never ever

used a knife before, Joe. Don't tell, Joe. Say you won't tell. There's a good guy. I always liked you, Joe. I stood up for you, too. Don't you remember? You won't tell, will you, Joe?"

The poor fellow dropped on his knees before Injun Joe.

"No, you've always been fair and square with me, Muff Potter. I won't go back on you. There, now, that's as fair as a man can say."

"Oh, Joe, you're an angel! I'll bless you for this the longest day I live."

"Come now, that's enough of that. This ain't no time for blubbering. You go one way. I'll go the other. Move now. Get out of here, Muff."

Potter trotted away. The Indian stood looking after him.

"He won't remember the knife till it's too late. He'll be too scared to come back for it. What an old fool!"

Chapter 9

Tom and Huck ran toward town as they had never run before. They looked over their shoulders from time to time, fearing they might be followed.

"If we can just get to the tanyard before we break down," whispered Tom. "I can't stand it much longer."

At last they did get there. They lay on the ground panting till they could again breathe easily.

"Huck, what do you reckon will come of this?" asked Tom.

"If Dr. Robinson dies, I reckon there'll be a hanging," said Huck.

Tom thought about that for a while.

"Who's going to tell, Huck? Us?"

"What are you talking about, Tom? Suppose Injun Joe *didn't* hang. He'd kill us sooner or later."

"That's what I was just thinking, Huck."

"If anybody tells, let Muff Potter do it, if he's fool enough. He's generally drunk enough."

"Huck, Muff Potter don't *know* it. How can he tell?"

"Why don't he know it?"

"Because he got that whack on his head when Injun Joe stabbed the doctor. He didn't *see* anything."

"That's so, Tom!"

"Besides, Huck, what if that whack killed him?"

"No, it ain't likely. He was drunk. When Pap's drunk, you could hit him with a church. You wouldn't faze him. It's the same with Muff Potter.

If he'd been sober it might have killed him."

"Huck, are you sure you can keep mum?"

"Tom, we *got* to keep mum. That Injun devil would as soon drown us as a pair of cats. If we squeal and they don't hang him, we're goners. Let's swear to each other—swear to keep mum."

"Right. That's the best thing to do. Let's do it right."

Tom picked up a clean pine shingle. He felt in his pocket for a pencil stub. By the light of the moon he scribbled this:

Huck Finn and Tom Sawyer swears they will keep mum about this and they wish they may drop down dead in their tracks if they ever tell and rot.

Tom unwound the thread from one of his needles. Each boy stuck his thumb and squeezed out a drop of blood. After lots of squeezes, Tom wrote a T.S. in blood. Then he showed Huck how to make an H and an F. They buried the shingle close to the wall.

While they were doing this, a dark form crept through a break in the other end of the building.

"Tom," whispered Huck, "does this keep us from *ever* telling—*always?*"

"Of course it does. It don't make any difference *what* happens. We got to keep mum. We'd drop down dead. Don't you know that?"

"Yes, I reckon that's so."

By and by a dog set up a long howl within ten feet of them. The boys grabbed each other in fright. That meant deep trouble for somebody.

"Which one of us does he mean?" asked Huck.

"I don't know. Peek through the crack. Quick!"

"No, *you,* Tom!"

"I can't. I can't *do* it, Huck!"

"Please, Tom. There it is again!"

"Oh, lordy, I'm thankful. That's Bruce Harbison's dog."

"Oh, that's good. I tell you, Tom, I was scared to death. I thought it was a *stray* dog. You know what it means when a *stray* dog howls at you."

The dog howled again. The boys' hearts sank once more.

"Oh, my! That ain't Harbison's dog," whispered Huck. "Do look, Tom!"

Tom was shaking, but he put his eye to the crack.

"Oh, Huck! It's a *stray* dog!"

"Quick, Tom, quick! Who does he mean?"

"Huck, he must mean us both. We're right together."

"Oh, Tom, I reckon we're goners."

"Look, Huck, look! He's got his *back* to us!"

"Well, he has! Now who can he mean?"

The howling stopped.

"Sh! What's that?" he whispered.

"Sounds like hogs grunting. No, it's somebody snoring."

"That *is* it! Where is it?"

"Down at the other end. Pap used to sleep there sometimes with the hogs."

"Huck, will you come look if I lead the way?"

"I don't like to. What if it's Injun Joe?"

At last they did go. They went tiptoeing down to the other end. They could see the snorer's face in the moonlight. It was Muff Potter. They tiptoed out of the building.

The dog howled again. They turned and saw the strange dog standing near Potter. Each boy went his way. Tom crept in at his bedroom window.

It was almost daylight. He undressed quickly, sure that nobody knew he'd been out. He didn't know that Sid had been awake for more than an hour.

When Tom woke, Sid was dressed and gone. Tom wondered why they hadn't called him for breakfast. He got dressed and went downstairs. The family was still at the table. They had finished breakfast long ago. Nobody said anything. Nobody looked at him.

After breakfast Aunt Polly took him aside. She asked him how he could break her old heart so. She said he was bringing her gray hairs with sorrow to the grave. It was no use, she said, to try to bring him up right. He begged her to forgive him. He promised again and again to do better. He could tell, though, that she didn't believe him.

He felt so bad he didn't think to pay Sid back for telling on him. He walked to school feeling gloomy and sad. He took his beating, along with Joe Harper, for playing hookey. He sat in his seat and let his head hang. He felt his elbow pressing against something hard. It was in a paper. He unrolled it. And then his heart did break. It was the brass door knob he had given to Becky!

Chapter 10

The whole town had news of the murder by noon. The story flew from one to another. The teacher let out school for the day.

A bloody knife had been found close to the murdered man. Somebody had said it belonged to Muff Potter. It was said that somebody had seen Potter washing himself in the creek about two o'clock in the morning. Potter had sneaked off. They had looked for him, but he had not been found. Horsemen were riding the nearby roads, looking for him.

The whole town, it seemed, had come to the graveyard. Tom went, too. Huck was there, too.

"Poor fellow! Poor young fellow!"

"This should be a lesson to grave robbers!"

"Muff Potter will hang for this!"

Now Tom shivered from head to toe. His eye fell on the stony face of Injun Joe.

Somebody cried, "It's him! It's him! He's coming himself!"

"Who? Who?" from twenty voices.

"Muff Potter!"

"He's stopped! Look out! Don't let him get away!"

"Ha!" said somebody. "He came back to look at what he'd done. I reckon he didn't expect any company."

The crowd stepped aside. The sheriff came leading Potter by the arm. When he stood before the murdered man, Potter got the shakes. He put his face in his hands. Then he burst into tears.

"I didn't do it, friends," he sobbed.

"Who said you did?" shouted a voice.

Potter looked around—and saw Injun Joe.

"Oh, Injun Joe, you promised me you'd never..."

"Is that your knife?" The sheriff held it before Potter's eyes. Potter would have fallen, but they caught him.

"Something told me to come back and—Go ahead, Joe. Tell them—"

Huck and Tom stared as that cold-hearted liar told his story. A little later, in court, Joe swore Muff Potter had killed the doctor.

"He must have sold out to the devil, Huck," said Tom. "If we keep an eye on him, maybe we'll see the devil."

But Tom's secret was an awful one. He had bad dreams every night for a week.

"Tom, you pitch around and talk in your sleep," said Sid. "You keep me awake half the time."

Tom got pale. He dropped his eyes.

"What have you got on your mind, Tom?" said Aunt Polly.

"Nothing." But his hand shook and he spilled his milk.

"You do talk such stuff," Sid said. "Last night you said, 'It's blood! It's blood!' You said that over and over. And you said, 'Don't hurt me, or I'll tell.' Tell what? What is it you'll tell?"

"Oh," said Aunt Polly, "it's that terrible murder. I dream about it most every night myself. Sometimes I dream it's me that done it."

Tom had another worry. Becky Thatcher had stopped coming to school. He began to hang around her father's house at night. She was ill, and he felt awful. What if she should die?

Tom started to get to school ahead of time. He hung around the gate of the schoolyard. He never played with the other boys. He was sick, he said. He looked it, too. He kept looking down the road. Jeff Thatcher would come into sight. Tom talked with him, hoping to get news of Becky. At last Tom would go into the schoolhouse and mope for the rest of the day.

But then one day she came. Tom's heart jumped with joy. The next minute he was out in the yard. He yelled. He laughed. He chased boys. He jumped over the fence. He stood on his head. All the while he kept an eye on Becky. But she kept looking the other way. He came closer. He snatched a boy's cap. He threw it on the schoolhouse roof. He burst into a bunch of boys, tumbling them left and right. He fell himself, almost under Becky's nose. She turned, with her nose in the air. He heard her say, "Some people think they're smart—always showing off!"

Tom's cheeks got red. He picked himself up and sneaked off.

Chapter 11

Tom now made up his mind. He felt gloomy and sad. He was a boy without friends. Nobody loved him. If they wanted to get rid of him, so be it. Yes, they had forced him to it at last. He would lead a life of crime. He would become a pirate.

Feeling like this, Tom met his friend, Joe Harper.

"I'm going to run away, Joe," he said. "Nobody wants me around any more. I hope you won't forget me. You've been a good friend."

It turned out that Joe felt the same way.

"I was just going to say the same thing to you," he said.

His mother had whipped him for something he didn't do. It was plain, he said, that she was tired of him. She wanted him to go. If she felt that way, there was nothing to do but go. He, too, was ready to run off.

The two friends agreed to stand by each other. They began to make plans. Joe was for being a hermit. After listening to Tom, though, he saw that a life of crime was better. He agreed to become a pirate.

There was an island about three miles below town. Nobody lived there. So they chose Jackson's Island for their camp. Then they hunted up Huckleberry Finn. He was glad to join them. They agreed to meet at a lonely spot on the river bank at midnight. There was a small log raft there that they meant to take. Each one was to bring fish hooks and lines. Each one was also to steal what he could.

About midnight Tom got there with a boiled ham. He whistled twice. Somebody answered with two whistles.

"Who goes there?" said a voice.

"Tom Sawyer, the Black Avenger of the Spanish Main. Say your names."

"Huck Finn, the Red Handed and Joe Harper, the Terror of the Seas."

"It is well. Give the password."

"Blood!"

The Terror of the Seas had brought a side of bacon. Finn the Red Handed had stolen a skillet and some tobacco. He'd also brought a few corncobs to make pipes with.

By and by they shoved off, with Tom in command. It took them about an hour to pass town on the raft. The Black Avenger stood still, with folded arms, looking his last on the place where he'd suffered. He wished SHE could see him now. The other pirates looked their last, too. They grounded the raft on the island about two o'clock in the morning. They took the sail from the raft and made a tent.

They built a fire at the edge of the woods. They cooked some bacon in Huck's frying pan. That was a lot of fun. They all agreed they would never go back. When the last slice of bacon was gone, they stretched out on the grass.

"Ain't this fun?" said Joe.

"It's great!" said Tom. "What would the boys say if they could see us?"

"Say? They'd just die to be here. Don't you think so, Huck?"

"I reckon so," said Huck. "Anyway, it suits *me* I don't want nothing better than this. I don't ever

get enough to eat in town. Nobody can come here and boss me around."

"It's just the life for me," said Tom. "You don't have to get up in the morning. You don't have to go to school. You don't have to work. You see a pirate don't have to do *anything*, Joe, when he's on shore. A hermit has to do a lot of praying. He don't have any fun, either. He's all by himself."

"Oh, yes. That's so," said Joe. "I hadn't thought much about it. I'd rather be a pirate, now that I've tried it."

"You see," said Tom, "people don't go much for hermits now. In the old days they did. But a pirate is always looked up to. A hermit has to sleep on the hardest place he can find. He has to put ashes on his head. He has to stand out in the rain."

"Why does he put ashes on his head?" said Huck.

"I don't know. But they got to do it. Hermits always do. You'd have to do that if you was a hermit."

"Darned if I would," said Huck.

"Why, Huck, you'd *have* to. How would you get around it?"

"I'd run away."

"Run away! Well, you would make a lousy hermit. You'd be a shame to the hermits."

By now Huck had scraped out a corncob. He fitted a weed stem to it. Then he loaded it up with tobacco and had a good smoke. The other two pirates wished they, too, knew how to smoke. Both made up their minds they were going to learn real soon.

"Say," said Huck, "what does a pirate have to do?"

"Oh, they have a great time," said Tom. "They

take ships and burn them. They get the money and bury it in awful places. They do that on islands where there's ghosts. They kill everybody in the ships. They make them walk a plank blindfolded."

"And they carry the women to the island," said Joe. "They don't kill the women."

"No," said Tom. "They don't kill the women. They're too noble to do that. And the women is always beautiful."

"And don't they wear the grandest clothes!" said Joe. "All gold and silver and full of diamonds!"

"Who?" said Huck.

"Why, the pirates," said Tom.

Huck looked sadly at his poor rags.

"I reckon I ain't dressed fit for a pirate," he said. "I ain't got none but these."

The other boys told him the fine clothes would come fast enough. They said Huck's clothes would be good enough to start out with.

"Most rich pirates do start out with fancy clothes," said Tom. "But you'll soon be rich, Huck."

They began to get sleepy. The pipe dropped from the fingers of the Red Handed. The Terror of the Seas and the Black Avenger had a harder time falling asleep. They said their prayers to themselves while lying down. There was nobody around, of course, to make them kneel. At first they weren't even going to say them. They didn't dare go that far. God might strike them dead if they did that.

They both now got a little worried. Had they done wrong to run away? What about the stolen meat? Of course they both had swiped apples and stuff before. But that they called "hooking" and it was not really wrong. Taking hams and bacon was plain, simple *stealing*. The Bible said they should not steal. They made up their minds that, as pirates, they'd "hook," but they wouldn't steal. At last they did fall asleep.

Chapter 12

When Tom woke in the morning, he wondered where he was. He sat up and rubbed his eyes. Then he remembered. He woke the other pirates. In a minute they were stripped and chasing one another in the water. A rise in the river had carried off their raft during the night.

They came back to camp feeling refreshed and hungry. They soon had the campfire burning again. Huck found a spring of clear, cold water close by. The boys made cups out of oak leaves and drank their fill. Joe began slicing bacon for breakfast. Tom and Huck threw out their fishing lines. Soon they were back with some handsome bass, some perch, and a small catfish. They fried the fish with the bacon. Never had food tasted so good. They found out that the faster you get fish on the fire, the better they taste.

They lay around in the shade after breakfast. Huck had a smoke. Then they went off in the woods. They found plenty of things to see. The island was about three miles long and a quarter mile wide. The Illinois shore was barely two hundred yards away. They took a swim about every hour. It was close to noon when they got back to camp.

Everything was still now. The boys began thinking. Pretty soon they began to feel—homesick! Even Finn the Red Handed started to dream about his doorsteps and barrels. The boys looked at one another. There was a long silence. Suddenly they heard a loud boom in the distance.

"What is *that?*" said Joe.

"I wonder," whispered Tom.

"It ain't thunder," said Huck, "because thunder—"

"Quiet!" said Tom. "Listen. Don't talk."

They waited a long time. Then the same boom sounded.

"Let's go and see."

They sprang to their feet. They ran to the shore facing toward the town. They parted the thick bushes and looked out over the water. The little steam ferryboat was about a mile below the town, drifting with the current. There were a great many skiffs out, too. They were rowing or floating near the ferryboat. The boys couldn't quite see what the men were doing. A moment later a big jet of white smoke burst from the ferryboat's side. The same dull boom sounded again.

"I know now!" cried Tom. "Somebody's drownded!"

"That's it!" said Huck. "They done that last summer when Bill Turner got drownded. They shoot a cannon over the water. That makes the drownded body come to the top. Yes, and they take loaves of bread along. They fill the bread loaves with quicksilver. Wherever there's a body, it will float right up to the bread."

"Yes, I've heard about that," said Joe. "I wonder what makes the bread do that."

"Oh, it ain't the bread so much," said Tom. "I reckon it's mostly what they *say* over it before they start it out."

"But they don't say anything over it," said Huck. "I've seen them. They don't."

"Well, that's funny," said Tom. "But maybe they say it to themselves. Of *course* they do.

Anybody might know that."

The other boys agreed that what Tom said made sense. You couldn't expect a dumb loaf of bread to know what to do.

"Say, I wish I was over there now," said Joe.

"I do too," said Huck. "I'd give heaps to know who it is."

The boys listened and watched. Suddenly Tom had a thought.

"Boys," he said, "I know who's drownded. It's us!"

The thought hit them like a bolt of lightning. They were heroes! They were missed! People were mourning for them! Tears were being shed for them! People were feeling sorry about them! The whole town was talking about them! It was worth while being a pirate, after all.

As darkness fell, the ferryboat steamed back to town. The skiffs, too, were soon gone. The pirates went back to camp. They were famous! They could hardly believe it. They caught fish and ate supper. They started to guess what people were saying about them. Tom wondered how SHE felt about him now. Was she crying because she had turned up her nose at him?

Tom and Joe could not help wondering about their families. Were they doing wrong? Should they let their folks keep on thinking they were dead? At last Joe spoke up.

"Do you suppose we'd better think about going back?" he said. "Maybe not right away, but—"

"Chicken!" cried Tom. "Joe wants his mother!"

Huck joined in with Tom. Of course, he had nobody to worry about *him*. Joe said he hadn't really meant it.

As the night went on, Huck began to nod. Soon

he was snoring. Joe followed next. Tom didn't move. He kept watching the other two. At last he got up on his knees. He felt around in the grass. He found two white pieces of bark. He knelt by the fire and wrote something on each piece. He rolled one up and put it in his jacket pocket. The other one he put in Joe's hat. He also put in the hat some of his things. They were a lump of chalk, a rubber ball, three fish hooks, and a glass marble. Then he tiptoed his way out among the trees. Soon he broke into a run toward the sand bar.

Chapter 13

A minute later Tom was wading toward the Illinois shore. When the current did not let him wade farther, he swam. He reached the shore at last. He struck out through the woods, his clothes dripping. About ten o'clock he came to an open place across from town. The ferryboat was there in the shadow of the trees. Tom crept down the bank. He slipped into the water. He swam a few strokes and climbed into the skiff lying on the ferryboat deck. He lay low.

Soon the bell rang.

"Cast off!" cried a voice.

Tom knew it was the ferryboat's last trip for the night. After fifteen minutes the wheels stopped. Tom slipped overboard. He swam ashore, landing about fifty yards downstream.

He ran down the empty streets and alleys. He soon came to his aunt's back fence. He climbed over and peeked into the sitting room window. There sat Aunt Polly, Sid, Mary, and Joe Harper's mother. They were by the bed. The bed was between them and the door. Tom went to the door. Softly he began to lift the latch. He pressed gently. The door opened a crack. He kept pushing. He got down on his knees and started to creep in.

"What makes the candle blow so?" said Aunt Polly. "Why, that door's open. Of course it is. How strange! Go shut it, Sid."

Tom made it under the bed just in time. He crept to where he could almost touch Aunt Polly's foot.

"But as I was saying," said Aunt Polly, "he wasn't a *bad* boy. Just full of fun and tricks. He never meant any harm. He was the most kind-hearted boy that ever was."

She began to cry.

"It was like that with my Joe," said Mrs. Harper. "Full of the devil. But he was fair and kind as he could be. To think I went and whipped that boy for something he didn't even do! Now I'll never see him again—never, never, never! That poor boy!"

Mrs. Harper sobbed as if her heart would break.

"I hope Tom's better off where he is," said Sid. "But if he'd been better in some ways—"

Aunt Polly looked angrily at Sid.

"Don't you say a word against my Tom, now that he's gone. God will take care of him. Don't you trouble yourself, sir! Oh, Mrs. Harper, I don't know how I can give him up! He was such a comfort to me. He nearly drove me crazy, but I did love that boy."

"Only last Saturday my Joe busted a firecracker right under my nose," said Mrs. Harper. "I knocked him off his feet. Little did I know how soon—. Oh, if it was to happen again, I'd hug him and bless him for it."

"Yes, yes, yes, I know just how you feel, Mrs. Harper. No longer ago than yesterday my Tom filled the cat with Painkiller. I thought that poor cat would tear the house down. God forgive me! I cracked Tom's head with my thimble. Poor boy! Poor dead boy! But he's out of all his troubles now. And the last words—"

That was too much for the old lady. She broke down sobbing. Tom could hear Mary crying. She, too, put in a good word for Tom from time to time.

Tom almost rushed out from under the bed to make her happy again. Almost, but not quite. Tom lay still.

He went on listening. It was thought that the boys had got drowned while taking a swim. A small raft had been missed. Some boys said that the missing boys had said the town would soon hear about them. They thought the boys had gone off on the raft. But the raft had been found. It was stuck on the Missouri shore five miles below town. This was Wednesday. If the bodies were still missing on Sunday, all hope would be gone. The funeral sermons would then be preached on Sunday.

Mrs. Harper, still sobbing, said good night. The two women threw themselves into each other's arms and wept. Aunt Polly said good night to Sid and Mary. They went off to bed. Aunt Polly then knelt down and prayed for Tom. There was so much love in her voice that Tom couldn't help crying.

He had to keep still long after she went to bed. She kept tossing in bed and turning over. At last she lay still, moaning in her sleep. Tom crept out from under the bed. He shaded the candlelight with his hand and stood looking down at her. He put his piece of bark by the candle. But then he thought of something. He put the bark back in his pocket. Then he bent over and kissed her pale lips. Then he left, latching the door behind him.

Back he went then to the ferry landing. Nobody was there. He walked boldly on board the ferryboat. The watchman was sound asleep. Tom untied the skiff tied to the boat. He jumped in. In another minute he was rowing upstream. He started to row across the river then. When he landed, he let the skiff drift. He stepped ashore and went into the woods. There he started on the home stretch. It was broad daylight before he came near the sand bar close to the camp. He rested till the sun was up high. He swam across to the island. A little later he walked into camp, dripping wet. Joe was talking.

"No," he said, "Tom is true blue, Huck. He will come back. He won't run off. He knows that would disgrace a pirate. Tom's too proud to leave us. He's up to something."

"How about the stuff he left for us?"

"They're not ours yet, Huck. The writing says they're ours if he ain't back here for breakfast."

"Which he is," said Tom, stepping grandly into camp.

They had a fine breakfast of bacon and fish. Tom told what had happened. They felt like heroes again when Tom finished. Tom lay down in the shade to sleep till noon.

Chapter 14

After dinner all the pirate gang hunted turtle eggs on the sand bar. They poked sticks into the sand. When they found a soft place they dug them out with their hands. Sometimes they would take fifty or sixty eggs out of one hole. They were round white things a little smaller than a walnut. They had a fine fried egg feast that night and another on Friday morning.

After breakfast they went whooping out on the sand bar. They chased one another round and round. As they ran, they threw off their clothes till they were naked. They splashed water in each other's faces and ducked one another.

When they were tired out they would run out and sprawl on the hot, dry sand. They like to cover themselves with the sand and wash it off in the water.

Next they got out their marbles and played "knucks" and "ringtaw" and "keeps." But that, too, got stale. They got to looking across the wide river to the town. Tom found himself writing BECKY on the sand with his big toe. He scratched it out and was angry with himself for his weakness. But then he wrote it again. He could not help it. He tried to bring the three of them together.

But Joe was feeling mighty low. He was so homesick he almost cried. Huck was gloomy, too. Tom was downhearted, but he tried hard not to show it. He had a secret which he was not ready to tell. He saw that he might have to bring it out to keep the others there.

"Oh, boys, let's give it up. I want to go home. It's so lonesome," said Joe.

"Oh, no, Joe! You'll feel better by and by," said Tom. "Just think of the fishing here."

"I don't care for fishing. I want to go home."

"But, Joe, there ain't such another swimming place anywhere."

"Swimming's no good. I don't seem to care for it, somehow. I mean to go home."

"Oh, shucks! Baby! You want to see your mother, I reckon."

"Yes, I *do* want to see my mother. You would, too, if you had one. I ain't any more baby than you."

"Well, we'll let the crybaby go home to his mother, *won't* we, Huck. Poor thing! Does it want to see its mother? And so it shall. *You* like it here, *don't* you, Huck? We'll stay, won't we?"

Huck said yes, but he didn't sound very happy about it.

"I'll never speak to you again as long as I live," said Joe. He moved away and started to dress.

"Who cares!" said Tom. "Nobody wants you to. Go home and get laughed at. Oh, you're a nice pirate! Huck and me ain't crybabies. We'll stay, won't we, Huck? Let him go if he wants to. I reckon we can get along without him."

But Tom was uneasy. Joe kept on dressing. A few minutes later he began to wade toward the Illinois shore. Tom's heart began to sink. He looked at Huck.

"I want to go, too, Tom," said Huck. "It was getting so lonesome. Now it'll be worse. Let's us go, too, Tom."

"I won't! You can all go, if you want to. I mean to stay."

"Tom, I better go."

"Well, go. Who's stopping you?"

"Tom, I wish you'd come, too. Now you think it over. We'll wait for you when we get to shore."

Tom ran after his friends yelling.

"Wait! Wait! I want to tell you something!"

They stopped and turned around. Tom then unfolded his secret. They listened. Slowly what he was saying dawned on them. They laughed and clapped their hands. They turned and went back to their games and sports. They kept talking about Tom's clever plan. After an egg and fish dinner, Tom wanted to learn to smoke. Joe said he'd like to learn, too. Huck made pipes and filled them. The boys had never smoked before.

Now they stretched themselves out on their elbows. They began to puff. The smoke had a nasty taste.

"Why, it's just as easy!" said Tom. "If I'd knowed it was this easy, I'd have learned long ago."

"So would I," said Joe. "It's nothing."

"Why, many times I've looked at people smoking," said Tom. "But I never thought I could do it."

"I believe I could smoke this pipe all day," said Joe. "I don't feel sick."

"Neither do I," said Tom. "I could smoke it all day, too."

So the talk went on. But soon there were long pauses in their chatter. They began to spit oftener. Both boys were looking pale now. Joe's pipe dropped from his fingers. Tom's did, too.

"I lost my knife," said Joe. "I better go find it."

"I'll help you," said Tom. "You go over that way. I'll hunt around the spring. No, you needn't come, Huck. We can find it."

So Huck sat down again. He waited for an hour. He went to find his friends. They were far apart in the woods. Both were very pale. Both were fast asleep.

They did not talk much at supper that night. Tom and Joe had a humble look. When Huck got his pipe ready, he started to fill theirs. They said no, they weren't feeling very well. They both said something they ate at dinner had disagreed with them.

Chapter 15

There was no joy in the little town that Saturday afternoon. The Harpers and Aunt Polly's family were in mourning. The townfolk talked very little. The children had no fun in their sports and games.

In the afternoon Becky Thatcher went back to the empty schoolyard.

"Oh, if I only had that brass door knob again. I haven't got anything to remember him by. I did love him so!"

She choked back a sob. She stopped.

"It was right here," she said. "Oh, if I could do it over again, I wouldn't say what I did. But he's gone now. I'll never, never see him again. Why was I so mean?"

She walked away with tears rolling down her cheeks. Some playmates, boys and girls, came by. They remembered things Tom and Joe had done and said.

When Sunday school was over the next morning, the church bell began to toll sadly. It was a very still Sunday. People started to come silently to church. They stopped here and there on the way to whisper about the sad happening. There was no talking inside the church, though. No one could remember when the little church had been so full before. Every bench was full.

Aunt Polly entered, followed by Sid and Mary. They were followed in turn by the Harper family, all dressed in black. All the people and the preacher stood up till they were seated on the front bench.

The preacher said a long prayer. The people sang a long, sad hymn. Then came the sermon. The preacher talked about the good things Tom and Joe had done. He told of the many time they had helped others, had been thoughtful. Here and there people began to cry. The preacher himself started to wipe his eyes as he went on and on.

There was a noise up in the empty balcony that nobody noticed. A moment later the church door creaked. The preacher raised his weeping eyes. His jaw dropped open. He stared. One by one the heads of people turned to see what the preacher was staring at. The three dead boys came marching up the aisle. Tom came first, Joe Harper came next, and Huck Finn brought up the rear. They had been hidden in the unused balcony, listening to their own funeral sermon!

Aunt Polly, Mary, and the Harpers threw themselves on Tom and Joe. They hugged them and kissed them. Poor Huck stood aside, not knowing what to do or where to hide. He started to sneak away, but Tom grabbed him.

"Aunt Polly," he said, "it ain't fair. Somebody's got to be glad to see Huck."

"And so they will!" cried Aunt Polly. "*I'm* glad to see him, poor motherless thing!"

Suddenly the preacher shouted at the top of his voice:

"Praise God from whom all blessings flow! *Sing!* And put your hearts in it!"

And sing they did. They made the rafters shake. Tom Sawyer the Pirate looked around. Every boy there was overcome with envy. Tom knew that this was the proudest moment of his life.

Chapter 16

That was Tom's secret—to attend their own funerals. Who ever has a chance to do that? They had paddled over to the Missouri shore on a log at dusk on Saturday. They landed five or six miles below the town. They had slept in the woods till nearly daylight. Then they had crept through back lanes and alleys to the church. They finished their sleep in the church balcony.

At breakfast Monday morning, Aunt Polly and Mary were very loving to Tom.

"Well," said Aunt Polly, "I don't say it wasn't a fine joke, Tom. You did keep everybody suffering a week while you had a good time. But why did you let *me* suffer so? You could have let me know that you weren't dead."

"Yes, you could have done that, Tom," said Mary. "You would have if you had thought of it, wouldn't you?"

"I—well, I don't know. It would have spoiled everything."

"Tom, I hoped you loved me that much," said Aunt Polly.

"Now, Aunt Polly," said Mary. "It's only Tom's way. He's always in such a rush he never thinks of anything."

"More's the pity," said Aunt Polly. "Sid would have thought of it. He would have done it, too."

"Now, Aunt Polly, you know I love you," said Tom.

"I'd know it better if you acted more like it."

67

"I wish I'd thought," said Tom. "I did dream about you. That's something, ain't it?"

"It ain't much. A cat does that much. But it's better than nothing. What did you dream?"

"Why, Wednesday night I dreamt you was sitting over there by the bed. Sid was sitting by the woodbox. Mary was next to him."

"Well, so we did. So we always do."

"And I dreamed Joe Harper's mother was here."

"Why, she *was* here! Did you dream any more?"

"Oh, lots. But it's so dim now."

"Well, *try* to remember. Can't you?"

"It seems to me that the wind—the wind blowed the—the—"

"Try harder, Tom. The wind did blow something. Come!"

Tom pressed his fingers to his forehead.

"I've got it now! It blowed the candle!"

"Mercy on us! Go on, Tom! Go on!"

"And it seems to me that you said, 'Why, I believe that door—"

"Go on, Tom!"

"Just let me study a moment. Oh, yes! You said you believed the door was open."

"As I'm sitting here, I did. Didn't I, Mary?"

"And then—and then—well, I can't be sure, but you made Sid go and—and—"

"Well? Well? What did I make him do?"

"Oh, you made him shut it."

"Well, for the land's sake! I never heard the beat of that in all my born days! Sereny Harper shall know about this before I'm an hour older! Go on, Tom!"

"Next you said I wasn't *bad,* but playful."

"And so it was. Well, goodness sakes! Go on, Tom!"

"And then you began to cry."

"So I did. So I did. And then—"

"Then Mrs. Harper started to cry. She said Joe was just the same. She wished she hadn't whipped him—"

"Go on, Tom."

"Then Sid, he said—he said—"

"I don't think I said anything," said Sid.

"Yes, you did, Sid," said Mary.

"Shut up, you two! Let Tom go on. What did he say, Tom?"

"I *think* he said he hoped I was better off where I was gone to. He said if I'd been better sometimes— "

"There! Did you hear that? It was his very words!"

"And you shut him up real quick."

"I'll say I did!"

"And Mrs. Harper told about Joe scaring her with a firecracker. Then you told about the cat and the Painkiller—"

"Just as true as I live!"

"And then there was a lot of talk about dragging the river for us. Oh, yes, about having the funeral on Sunday. Then you and Mrs. Harper hugged and cried. Then she went home."

"It happened just so! It happened just so, as sure as I'm sitting here. Tom, you couldn't have told it more like if you'd seen it. And then what? Go on, Tom."

"Then I thought you prayed for me. I could see you. I could hear every word you said. You went to bed. I was so sorry. I took and wrote on a piece of bark. It said, 'We ain't dead. We are only off being pirates.' I put it on the table by the candle. You looked so good laying there asleep, I thought

I leaned over and kissed you on the lips."

"Did you, Tom? Did you? I forgive you everything for that!"

She grabbed Tom and hugged him and kissed him. Tom felt like a heel.

"It was very kind," said Sid, "even though it was a dream."

"Shut up, Sid! A body does the same in a dream as when he's awake. Here's a big red apple. I've been saving it for you, Tom. I kept it in case you was ever found again. Now go on to school. I'm thankful to the good God and Father of us all that I've got you back. Go on Sid, Mary, Tom."

Chapter 17

The children left for school. Aunt Polly went to call on Mrs. Harper. She could not wait to tell her about Tom's wonderful dream. Sid did not say what he thought: "Pretty hard to believe. A long dream with no mistakes in it!"

Tom had become a hero. He acted as if he didn't hear people talk about him. He did, though, and the talk was like food and drink to him. The smaller boys flocked at his heels. They were proud to be seen by him. Boys his own age pretended he hadn't been gone. They were green with envy, though.

At school the children made a big fuss over Tom and Joe. The two heroes soon became quite stuck up. They told about their adventures again and again. At last, when they got out their pipes and smoked, they reached the peak of their glory.

Tom now made up his mind to show Becky Thatcher who was boss. She needed him more than he needed her. Now that he was famous, she would want to make up. Well, he meant to teach her a lesson. When she came to school, Tom pretended not to see her. He moved over to some boys and girls and started to talk to them. He saw that she was pretending to have a good time with her friends. She kept coming closer and closer to him. He just looked the other way. Tom now started to talk with Amy Lawrence. Of course Becky didn't like *that*. She spoke to a girl standing almost at Tom's elbow.

"Why, Mary Austin! You bad girl, why didn't you come to Sunday school?"

"I did come. Didn't you see me?"

"Why, no! Did you? Where did you sit?"

"I was in Miss Peter's class. That's where I always go. I saw *you*."

"Did you? Why, that's funny. I didn't see you. I wanted to tell you about the picnic."

"Oh, how nice! Who's going to give it?"

"My ma's going to let me have one."

"Oh, goody! I hope she'll let *me* come."

"Well, she will. The picnic's for me. She'll let anybody come that I want. I want you to come."

"That's ever so nice. When is it going to be?"

"By and by. Maybe when school lets out."

"Oh, won't it be fun! Are you going to have all the girls and boys?"

"Yes, everyone that's friends with me—or wants to be."

She glanced at Tom. But Tom just kept on talking to Amy Lawrence.

"Oh, may I come?" asked Grace Miller.

"Yes."

"And me?" asked Sally Rogers.

"Yes."

"And me too?" said Susy Harper. "And Joe?"

"Yes."

And so on it went. Soon all the boys and girls there had begged to come to the picnic. All, that is, but Tom and Amy. Tom turned coolly away, still talking. He took Amy with him. Becky's lips trembled. Tears came to her eyes. She went on chattering, but her heart was not in it. She got away as soon as she could. She hid herself and had a good cry. Then she sat with her broken pride till the bell rang.

72

At recess Tom kept on flirting with Amy. But Becky now had a plan, too. She was sitting on a bench behind the schoolhouse. With her was Alfred Temple. They had their heads together, looking at a picture book. That did it for Tom. He began to hate himself for not making up with Becky. He called himself a fool and all the hard names he could think of. Amy chatted on, happy as a lark. But now Tom lost interest in her. He didn't listen to what she said any longer. He kept drifting to the back of the school to stare at Becky and Alfred. Becky never looked at him. She knew she was winning her fight now. She was glad to see Tom suffer. After all, he had made her suffer.

Tom told Amy he had things to do, so he left her standing.

"Any other boy!" said Tom, gritting his teeth. "Any boy in the whole town but that St. Louis smarty! Oh, all right. I licked you the first day you came to town. I'll lick you again! You just wait till I catch you out! I'll—"

Tom went home at noon. Becky and Alfred sat together again. When Tom did not come back, she lost interest in Alfred. She began to wish she hadn't carried out her plan so far. Poor Alfred saw that he was losing her.

"Oh, here's a nice one! Look at this picture, Becky," he would say.

"Oh, don't bother me!" Becky cried. "I don't care about those old pictures."

She burst into tears, got up, and walked away. Alfred tried to comfort her.

"Go away!" she cried. "Leave me alone! I hate you!"

Alfred wondered what he had done. He was angry. At last the truth dawned on him. The girl had used him to spite Tom Sawyer! He wished he could get Tom into trouble. Tom's spelling book lay on his desk. Alfred opened the book to the lesson for the afternoon. He poured ink all over the page.

Becky happened to look in through the window as Alfred poured the ink. She started to go home. She thought she would find Tom and tell him what Alfred had done. Tom would thank her and they would make up. In another minute she changed her mind. She remembered how Tom had acted about the picnic. The thought filled her with shame. She made up her mind to let him get whipped and to hate him forever.

Chapter 18

Tom came home feeling bad. Aunt Polly didn't make him feel any better.

"Tom, I ought to skin you alive!" she said.

"Auntie, what have I done?"

"Well, you've done enough. Here I go over to Sereny Harper, like an old softie. I think I'm going to make her believe that rubbish about your dream. She'd found out from Joe that you'd been over here that night. You heard all that talk we had that night. Tom, I don't know what's to become of you. It makes me feel so bad. You let me go over there and make a fool of myself. You never said a word. Shame on you!"

Tom hadn't thought of that. He had thought he was being clever about the dream. His joke now seemed mean and shabby. He hung his head. He couldn't think of anything to say.

"Auntie," he said at last, "I wish I hadn't done it. I didn't think."

"Oh, child, you never think. You never think of anything but yourself. You could come all the way over here from Jackson's Island to laugh at our sorrow. You fooled me with a lie about a dream. You wouldn't think to pity us and save us from sorrow."

"Auntie, I know now it was mean. But I didn't mean to be mean. I didn't, honest. I didn't come over here to laugh at you that night."

"What did you come for then?"

"To tell you not to be uneasy about us. To tell

you we hadn't been drownded."

"Tom, Tom, I would be happy if I could believe that. You know you never did that. I know it, too, Tom."

"I did, Auntie! I did. I wish I may never stir, if I didn't."

"Oh, Tom, don't lie. Don't do it. It only makes things a hundred times worse."

"It ain't a lie, Auntie. It's the truth. I wanted to keep you from sorrowing. That was all that made me come."

"I'd give the whole world to believe that. It would cover up a lot of sins, Tom. I'd almost be glad you ran off and acted so bad. But it makes no sense. Why didn't you tell me, then?"

"Why, you see when you talked about the funeral, I got full of the idea of hiding in the church. I couldn't bear to spoil it. So I put the bark back in my pocket and kept mum."

"What bark?"

"The bark I had wrote on to tell you we were pirates. I wish now you'd waked up when I kissed you. I do—honest."

The hard lines in Aunt Polly's face got soft.

"Did you kiss me, Tom?"

"Why, yes. I did."

"Are you sure you did, Tom?"

"Why, yes. I did, Auntie."

"Why did you kiss me, Tom?"

"Because I loved you so. You laid there moaning in your sleep. I was so sorry for you."

The words sounded true. The old lady's voice shook when she spoke.

"Kiss me again, Tom. And be off with you to school."

The moment he was gone she ran to the closet.

She got out the torn old jacket Tom wore as a pirate. Then she stopped. She spoke to herself.

"No, I don't dare. Poor boy! I reckon he's lied about it. I hope the Lord—I *know* the Lord will forgive him. It was so kind of him to lie. But I don't want to find out it's a lie. I won't look."

She put the jacket away. She stood there for a while thinking. Twice she pulled her hand back. She reached again.

"It's a good lie. I won't let it get me down."

And so she felt in the jacket pocket. A moment later she was reading Tom's piece of bark. The tears of thanks flowed from her eyes.

"I could forgive the boy now," she said, "if he committed a million sins!"

Chapter 19

When Tom went on to school, he happened to meet Becky Thatcher. He ran right up to her.

"I acted mighty mean today, Becky," he said. "I'm sorry. I won't ever act that way again as long as I live. Please make up, won't you?"

Becky stopped. She looked at Tom angrily.

"I'll thank you to keep to yourself, Tom Sawyer. I'll never speak to you again."

She tossed her head back and walked on. Tom was stunned. He didn't even say, "Who cares, Miss Smarty?" He was upset and angry, though. He wished she was a boy so he could give her a good licking. When he passed her later, he did make a nasty remark. She did, too. Becky could hardly wait for school to start. The teacher would see Tom's speller and give him a good whipping. She wasn't about to tell on Alfred Temple now.

Poor girl, she did not know she would soon be in trouble herself. The schoolmaster, Mr. Dobbins, was an unhappy man. He had always wanted to be a doctor. Being too poor to do that, he had to become a teacher. Every day he took out a book from his desk. He would read it when his pupils were busy doing their written work. He kept that book under lock and key. Every child in school wanted to see what was in that book. The chance never came. Now, as Becky was passing by his desk, she saw that the key was in the desk lock! She glanced around. She was alone. In a moment she had the book in her hands. The word

ANATOMY on the cover meant nothing to her. She began to turn the pages. She came to a big colored picture of a naked human. At that moment a shadow fell on the page. Tom Sawyer had stepped in the door. He caught a quick look at the picture. Becky snatched at the book to close it. She had the bad luck to tear the page down the middle. She pushed the book into the desk. Then she turned the key and burst out crying.

"Tom Sawyer, you're as mean as you can be," she cried. "You sneaked up to see what I was doing!"

"How could I know you was looking at anything?" said Tom.

"You ought to be ashamed, Tom Sawyer! You know you're going to tell on me. What shall I do? Oh, what shall I do? I'll be whipped. I never was whipped in school!"

Then she stamped her foot.

"*Be* so mean if you want to," she said. "I know something else that's going to happen. You just wait and you'll see! Hateful! Hateful! Hateful!"

Tom stood and scratched his head helplessly.

"What a strange kind of a fool a girl is," he said to himself. "Never been licked in school! Shucks. What's a licking? That's just like a girl. They're so thin skinned! They're chicken! Of course I ain't going to tell old Dobbins on this little fool. But what of it? Old Dobbins will ask who tore his book. Nobody will answer. Then he'll do what he always does. He'll ask one, then another. When he comes to the right girl, he'll know it. Girls' faces always tell on them. They ain't got any backbone. She'll get licked. Well, it's a tight place for Becky Thatcher. There ain't no way out of it. Well, she'd liked to see me in such a fix. Let her sweat it out."

Tom joined the boys and girls outside. In a few minutes the schoolmaster came and school started. Every time Tom looked, Becky's face troubled him. He did not want to feel sorry for her, but he couldn't help it. Soon the ink was discovered in Tom's spelling book. Tom took his whipping like a man. Becky thought she would be glad to see Tom whipped. She wasn't, though. She felt like telling on Alfred Temple, but she didn't. She kept her mouth shut because she thought Tom would tell on her.

Tom took his whipping and went back to his seat. He thought he might have spilled the ink himself.

A whole hour drifted by. The master sat nodding at his desk. By and by Mr. Dobbins yawned. Then he unlocked his desk. He slowly reached for his book. The pupils looked up lazily. But two of them watched him very carefully. Tom shot a quick look at Becky. She had the look of a hunted rabbit in a trap. Mr. Dobbins took the book out. He settled himself to read. The next moment the master faced the school. Every eye sank before his look.

"Who tore this book?"

There was not a sound. You could have heard a pin drop. The master looked at one face after another, looking for signs of guilt.

"Benjamin Rogers, did you tear this book?"

"No."

"Joseph Harper, did you?"

"No, sir."

The master turned to look at the girls.

"Amy Lawrence?"

A shake of the head.

"Grace Miller?"

"No, sir."

"Susan Harper, did you do this?"

"No."

The next girl was Becky Thatcher. Tom looked at her pale, frightened face.

"Rebecca Thatcher, did you tear—no, look me in the face. Did you tear this book?"

A thought shot like lightning through Tom's brain. He sprang to his feet.

"I done it!" he shouted.

The whole school stared in wonder at Tom. Had he lost his mind? Tom stepped forward to take his beating. The love that shone from Becky's eyes would have paid for a hundred beatings. Without a cry he took the worst whipping Mr. Dobbins had ever given. Tom was also ordered to stay two hours after school. Tom didn't mind. He knew who would be waiting for him outside. She was there.

Tom went to bed planning to pay Alfred Temple for spilling ink on his speller. Becky had told him all. He fell asleep with Becky's latest words lingering in his ears—

"Tom, how *could* you be so noble!"

Chapter 20

School was almost over for the summer. The schoolmaster, always mean, grew meaner. He wanted the school to make a good showing on Exam Day. On that last night the whole town would come to the schoolhouse. The pupils would learn speeches, read poems, and show off. The younger pupils now lived in daily fear at school. The whippings came oftener and longer. Mr. Dobbins was still a strong man. He was completely bald under his wig, but he had only reached middle age. The smaller boys spent lots of time planning to get even with him. Most of their plans didn't work out.

At last they hit upon a plan that might work. They got the sign painter's boy to help. He had his own reasons for helping. The master boarded with his father's family. Mr. Dobbins had often given the boy reason to hate him. The master's wife was going to leave town for a few days. That would help the plan work. The master always got ready for big days by getting himself tanked up. The sign painter's boy said that he'd do his part when Dobbins napped in his chair after supper. Then he would wake the master in time to get to school.

Exam Day finally came. At eight o'clock in the evening the school was brightly lit. There were flowers everywhere. The desks were scrubbed. The floor had been sanded. The master was seated in his great chair on a raised platform. Behind him was the blackboard, also scrubbed clean of chalk dust. Three long rows of benches on each side and six rows in front were filled with big shots and parents. To the left was another big platform. Here were seated the pupils who were to perform. The rest of the big room was filled with pupils who had no parts.

The smaller boys and girls did their parts first. Tom Sawyer had the "Give me liberty or give me death" speech to recite. He started like a house afire, but broke down in the middle of it. Tom tried, but he couldn't finish. He sat down in disgrace. A few kind people clapped hands for him.

Pupil after pupil followed. The bigger boys and girls had written their own papers. Some had written poems. Hour after hour they read them from the platform. After each one the people clapped their hands wearily. The pupils blushed, bowed, and found their seats.

Now the master, still feeling pretty good from his early drinking, set his chair aside. He turned his back to the people and started to draw a map on the blackboard. The geography class came forward, ready to answer questions.

The master's hand was shaking some and he was making a mess of the map. He erased lines and drew in new ones. Some of the parents began to giggle. He worked hard and began to get it right. But now the giggling grew louder.

Right over the master's head was an opening in the ceiling. Out of this opening, hanging by a fishing line around its belly, came a cat. It had a rag tied around its head to keep it from mewing. As it came lower and lower, it clawed the air wildly. The laughing grew louder. Inch by inch the boy in the attic lowered the clawing cat. The cat grabbed Mr. Dobbins' wig in her claws. Instantly

the boy in the attic yanked the cat—and the wig—
out of sight!

How the lights did shine on the schoolmaster's
bald head! The sign painter's boy had gilded it
with golden paint while Dobbins was napping
after supper!

That broke up the meeting. The boys got even
with the schoolmaster at last.

Chapter 21

At last Muff Potter's murder trial came on in the court. The town could talk of nothing else. Tom could not get away from it. It kept him in a cold shiver. He took Huck to a lonely place to talk.

"Huck, have you ever told anybody about—you know what?"

"About what?"

"You know what."

"Oh. Of course I haven't."

"Never a word?"

"Not a word, so help me. What makes you ask?"

"Well, I was scared."

"Why, Tom Sawyer, we wouldn't be alive two days if that got found out. *You* know that."

"Huck, they couldn't get you to tell, could they?"

"Get me to tell? If I wanted that devil Joe to drown me, I'd tell."

"Well, I reckon we're safe as long as we keep mum. But let's swear again."

"I agree."

So they swore again.

"What are folks saying, Huck?"

"Well, it's just Muff Potter all the time. It makes me want to hide."

"I reckon he's a goner. Don't you feel sorry for him sometimes?"

"Most always. He ain't worth much. But then he ain't done anything to hurt anybody. Just fishes a little to get money to get drunk on. Loafs around town. But he's kind of good. He give me

half a fish once when there wasn't enough for two. Lots of times he's stood by me when I was out of luck."

"Well, he's fixed kites for me, Huck. I wish we could get him out of there."

"We couldn't get him out, Tom. It wouldn't do any good. They'd just ketch him again."

"Yes—so they would. But I hate to hear them bad mouth him when he never did—you know what."

"I do too, Tom. I hear them call him a bloody killer. They wonder why he wasn't hung long ago."

"Yes, they talk like that all the time. They say if he was to get free, they'd lynch him."

"And they'd do it, too."

The boys did what they had often done before. They went to the jail window and gave Potter tobacco and matches. He was on the ground floor. There were no guards.

"You've been mighty good to me, boys," he said. "Better than anybody else in this town. I don't forget it. The others forget old Muff when he's in trouble. But Tom and Huck don't. *They* don't forget him. Well, boys, I done an awful thing. I was drunk at the time. That's the only way I can explain it. Now I got to hang for it, and that's right and fair. What I want to say is this: don't ever get drunk. Stick your hands in so I can shake 'em. Those hands have helped Muff Potter. They'd help him more if they could."

Tom went home feeling bad. He had terrible dreams that night. The next two days he hung around the courtroom. Huck was there, too. They didn't look at each other. The news was always bad. The law was closing in on Muff Potter. At the end of two days everybody thought that Injun Joe's story was true. There was no question as to what the jury would do.

Tom was out late that night. He came in through the window. It was hours before he got to sleep. The whole town flocked to the courthouse the next morning. This was to be the great day. After a long wait the jury came in and sat in their places. A little later they brought Potter in. He looked scared and hopeless. Injun Joe was there, stony faced as ever. Then the judge came in.

Now a witness was called. He said he had seen Muff Potter washing in the creek. He said Muff had sneaked away. The lawyer then said:

"Take the witness."

"I have no questions to ask him," said Muff's lawyer.

The next witness said he had seen the knife near the doctor's body.

"Take the witness."

"I have no questions to ask him," said Muff's lawyer.

A third witness swore he had often seen Potter use the knife.

"Take the witness."

"No questions," said Muff's lawyer again. The people didn't like that. Did that lawyer mean to let Potter hang without doing anything?

Two or three witnesses then said Potter had said he was guilty at the grove. Again Muff's lawyer asked them no questions.

Everything that happened was brought out by witnesses. None of the witnesses were cross questioned by Potter's lawyer. The people grumbled again. The judge had to tell them to be quiet.

"By the oaths of these witnesses we have proved

that the prisoner is guilty of this awful crime," said the lawyer. "We rest our case."

Poor Potter groaned. He put his face in his hands. He rocked softly back and forth. Muff's lawyer rose and faced the jury.

"Your honor," he said, "we were going to prove that the prisoner did the crime while he was drunk. We have changed our mind. We will now prove that he did not do the crime. Call Thomas Sawyer to the witness stand."

Every face in the room showed surprise. Even Potter was surprised. Every eye fastened on Tom. He rose and went to the witness stand. There he swore to tell the truth, the whole truth, and nothing but the truth.

"Thomas Sawyer, where were you on the seventeenth of June, about the hour of midnight?"

Tom looked at Injun Joe's iron face. The words wouldn't come at first. After a few moments, though, he could be heard.

"In the graveyard."

"A little louder, please. Don't be afraid. You were—where?"

"In the graveyard."

"Were you anywhere near Hoss Williams' grave?"

"Yes, sir."

"Speak up. How near were you?"

"As near as I am to you."

"Were you hidden, or not?"

"I was hid."

"Where?"

"Behind the elm trees on the edge of the grave."

"Anyone with you?"

"Yes, sir. I went there with—"

"Wait. Never mind. We'll bring him out at the

right time. Did you carry anything there with you?"

"Only a—a—dead cat."

"We will show you the bones of that cat," said Muff's lawyer. "Now tell us everything that happened. Tell it in your own words. Don't be afraid."

Tom began slowly at first. But as he warmed up the words flowed better. Every eye was fixed on Tom. He told it all. At the end he said, "—as the doctor knocked Muff out with the board, Injun Joe jumped up with the knife and—"

Crash! Quick as lightning, Joe sprang for a window. In another moment he was gone.

Chapter 22

Tom Sawyer was a hero again. The old folks patted his head and said he had been a brave boy. His young friends were green with envy. He must have told his story a hundred times to them. Of course Becky Thatcher was eager to hear it again and again. Tom's name got into print, too. The town newspaper made a big fuss over him. Mary cut out the stories about Tom and saved them. Aunt Polly was proud of him.

"You told the truth, Tom" she said as she hugged him. "Bless you, my boy!" She said Tom would probably become President of the United States if he could escape hanging.

People now were kind to Muff Potter. The ones who had wanted to lynch him were now proud to shake his hand. He was invited for meals and offered places to sleep. When he was too shy to accept, they agreed that he was a drunken bum after all. And, of course, he was a grave robber, wasn't he? Muff nearly cried when he met Tom. He could not thank him enough for saving his life.

Tom felt fine during the daytime. People often stopped him on the street to praise him. The town folks pointed him out to strangers or visitors. Tom's nights, though, were awful for a long time. He had a hard time getting to sleep. He lay awake for hours, long after Sid began snoring. When he did doze off, he had horrible dreams about Injun Joe. The law men had searched the state for Joe. He had not been seen again. Tom stopped going out after dark for fear of Injun Joe.

Tom had been unable to get Muff Potter and the murder out of his mind. He knew that it had been wrong to swear to keep mum about the murder and let Muff hang. He had gone, late at night, to Muff Potter's lawyer. He had told him the whole story. That made him feel a lot better. He had to admit to Huck that he had broken their oath. Huck never did get over his terror of Injun Joe. In spite of his fear, he agreed to back up Tom's story. He was even willing to take the witness stand himself. He *was* glad that Joe had escaped before finding out that he, Huck, had been in the graveyard that night. Muff's lawyer later promised to keep mum about Huck's part in the adventure. It had not been necessary to get into the witness stand at the trial. The trial ended when Joe escaped.

As the days passed into months, the boys' fear slowly began to fade. Before too long, then, even Injun Joe didn't keep them awake at night.

Chapter 23

Everybody who has read pirate stories knows there must be a lot of buried treasure just waiting to be found. Tom Sawyer knew it. He soon had Huck Finn believing it, too. The trouble was they didn't know *where* to look. Tom said pirates and robbers liked to bury their gold under big trees. That made it easy to find the place again when they came back for it. Tom knew where a very tall old tree stood. Armed with picks and spades, they tried digging there. They found no treasure. Next they tried digging under an old tree on Cardiff Hill, behind the Widow Douglas' house. Again, no treasure.

"Say, Tom, let's give this place up. Let's try somewheres else," said Huck.

"All right. I reckon we better."

"Where will it be?"

"I know!" cried Tom. "Let's try the haunted house!"

"I don't like haunted houses, Tom. You know there's ghosts that hang around at night."

"Yes, that's so. But they don't come around in the daytime. We needn't be scared."

"Well, all right. We'll try the haunted house if you say so."

The haunted house stood alone. The fences had fallen long ago. Weeds grew right up to the doorstep. The window sashes were empty. A corner of the roof had caved in. They crept to the door and looked inside. They saw a weed-grown,

floorless room. There was an old fireplace. A broken set of stairs led to the second floor. Cobwebs hung everywhere. The boys tiptoed in and spoke in whispers. They tossed their picks and spades aside and climbed the rickety stairs. There wasn't anything up there, either. They were about to come down when Tom heard something.

"Sh!" he whispered.

"What is it?" whispered Huck. His voice shook.

"There! Hear it?"

"Yes! Let's run!"

"Keep still! Don't move! They're coming right toward the door!"

The boys stretched themselves out on the floor. They peeked through cracks in the planks.

"They've stopped. No, they're coming. Here they are! Don't whisper another word, Huck."

Two men came in. One was the deaf-and-dumb Spaniard who had come to town lately. The other man was a stranger. He wore rags and had a mean-looking face. The Spaniard was wrapped in a blanket. He had bushy white whiskers. Long white hair hung from under his hat. He wore dark green glasses. When they came in, the mean-looking fellow was talking in a low voice. They sat on the ground, facing the door. The boys could hear him clearly.

"No," he said. "I've thought it all over. I don't like it. It's too much of a risk."

"Risk?" said the "deaf-and-dumb" Spaniard— to the surprise of the boys.

"You're chicken!"

The voice scared the boys almost to death. It was Injun Joe's voice!

"What's riskier than that job up north? Nothing has come of that."

"That one was different. There wasn't another house nearby. Nobody will know we tried. We just didn't make it."

"Well, what's riskier than coming here in the daytime? Anybody would wonder if they saw us."

"I know that. But there wasn't any place as handy. I want to get out of here. I wanted to yesterday, but those darn kids was playing on the hill in plain sight."

The two men then got out some food and ate.

"Look here, lad," said Injun Joe. "You go back up the river where you belong. Wait there till you hear from me. I'll take my chances on dropping into this town once more. We'll do that risky job when I get there. Then off we'll go to Texas."

Both men soon started yawning.

"I'm dead for sleep," said Joe. "It's your turn to watch."

He lay down in the weeds. Soon he began to snore. By and by the watcher began to nod. His head drooped. He, too, began to snore.

The boys took a deep breath.

"Now's our chance! Come!" said Tom.

"I can't," said Huck. "I'd die if they was to wake."

At last Tom rose slowly and softly. But the first step he took caused the floor board to creak loudly. He sank back, scared to death. He didn't try again.

Now one snore stopped. Injun Joe sat up, stared, and smiled. He kicked his partner.

"A fine watchman *you* are! All right, though. Nothing's happened."

"Have I been asleep?"

"Yes. It's nearly time to be moving. What shall we do with the little loot we've got left?"

"I don't know. Let's leave it here. No use to take

it away till we go to Texas. Six hundred and fifty in silver is too heavy to carry."

"Well, all right. We can come here once more. Let's bury it—and bury it deep."

"Right!" The fellow walked across the room. He knelt down. He raised a flat floor stone. He took out a bag full of coins. He took out thirty dollars for himself and thirty for Joe. Then he handed the bag to Joe. Joe was on his knees in the corner, digging with his knife.

The boys forgot their fears. With shining eyes they watched. Luck! Six hundred dollars was enough to make half a dozen boys rich!

Joe's knife struck something.

"What is it?" asked the other fellow.

"A rotten plank. No, it's a box, I think. Here, help me. Never mind. I've broke a hole in it." He reached his hand in and pulled out—

"Man, it's money!"

The two men looked carefully at the coins. They were gold. The boys' eyes shone—here truly was buried treasure!

"We'll make short work of this," said Joe's friend. "I saw some picks and spades over there in the corner."

He ran and brought the boys' picks and spades. Injun Joe took a pick. He looked at it carefully. He shook his head and muttered to himself. He began to dig. The box was not very big. It was bound in iron and had once been a very strong one. The men looked happily at the shining gold coins.

"Partner," said Joe, "there's thousands of dollars here."

"I always heard that Murrel's gang was around here one summer," said the stranger.

"I know it," said Joe. "This looks like their

stuff."

"*Now* you won't need to do that other job in town."

"You don't know me," said Joe. "That ain't just robbery. It's revenge! I'll need your help. When it's done—then Texas. Go home till you hear from me."

"Well, if you say so. What'll we do with this? Bury it again?"

"No! I nearly forgot. That pick had fresh dirt on it. Who brought those tools here? Where are the people? Have you heard or seen anybody? No. We'll have to take it to my den."

"Why, of course! You mean Number One?"

"No. Number Two. Under the cross. The other place is too easy to find."

"All right. It's nearly dark enough to start."

Injun Joe looked out the windows.

"Who could have brought those tools here?" he said. "Do you reckon they can be upstairs?"

The boys stopped breathing. Injun Joe put his hand on his knife. He turned toward the stairway. The boys thought of hiding in the closet, but they were too scared to move. Joe started up the stairs, knife in hand. Suddenly there was a crash of rotten timbers. Joe landed on the ground. The planks of the ruined stairway lay scattered around him. He got up cursing.

"Well," said Joe's friend, "if anybody's up there, let them *stay*. Who cares? It will be dark in ten minutes. Let them follow us if they want to."

Shortly afterward they slipped out of the house. They moved toward the river with their box.

Tom and Huck stared after them through cracks between the logs. Follow? Not they! They were glad to reach ground safely. They felt bad about bringing in the tools. Were it not for those tools, Injun Joe would have hidden the silver with the gold in the haunted house.

They agreed to keep an eye on that so-called Spaniard. He was going to get revenge on somebody. They might be able to follow him to "Number Two."

"Huck," said Tom. "Revenge? What if he means *us*?"

Huck nearly fainted. They talked it all over. As they came to town they agreed that Joe *might* want revenge on somebody else. Or maybe he meant only Tom. Huck had never gone on the witness stand. Muff Potter's lawyer had kept mum about Huck's being at the graveyard. Of course that didn't make Tom feel any better.

Chapter 24

After breakfast Tom went to find Huck. Huck was sitting on a flatboat with his feet hanging in the water. What had happened yesterday seemed like a dream to Tom.

"Tom," said Huck, "if we hadn't brought those tools in the haunted house, we'd have got the money. Ain't it awful?"

"It ain't a dream, then. I almost wish it was."

"Dream? If them stairs hadn't broke down, you'd seen how much dream it was! I've had dreams enough about that Spanish devil."

"Huck, we've got to *find* him. We've got to track that money."

"Tom, we'll never find him. You get only one chance to win that much money. We lost it. I'd feel mighty shaky if I was to see him."

"Well, he scared me, too, Huck. But I'd like to find his Number Two."

"Number Two—yes. I can't make any sense out of that. What do you reckon it is?"

"I don't know. Maybe it's the number of a house."

"No, Tom, that ain't it. Not in this one-horse town. There ain't no house numbers here."

"Well, that's so. Let me think. Maybe it's the number of a room—maybe a room in a tavern."

"That's it! We got only two taverns. We can find out quick."

"You stay here, Huck. Wait till I come back."

Tom was off at once. He was gone a half hour.

In the best tavern No. Two was rented by a young lawyer. In the other tavern's No. Two something was strange. The tavern keeper's young son told Tom it was always locked. He never saw anybody go in or come out except at night. He said he had seen a light in there the night before.

"That's what I found out, Huck. I reckon that's the Number Two we're after."

"I reckon it is, Tom. Now what are we going to do?"

"The back door of that Number Two opens to the alley between the tavern and the old brick store. Now you get hold of all the door keys you can find. I'll swipe Aunt Polly's. The first dark night we'll try 'em. Keep an eye out for Injun Joe. He said he was going to get his revenge. If you see him, follow him. If he don't go to that Number Two, we'll know that ain't the place."

That night Tom and Huck hung around the tavern till after nine. One watched the alley. One watched the tavern door. Nobody entered the alley or left it. The "Spaniard" did not show up. Tom and Huck then went to bed. Tuesday and Wednesday brought the same bad luck. On Thursday night Tom slipped out with Aunt Polly's old tin lantern. He also brought a towel to blindfold it with. An hour before midnight the tavern closed and the lights were put out. Injun Joe had not been seen. Nobody had gone into the alley or had come out. The thunder sounded in the distance.

Tom lit his lantern. He wrapped the towel around it. The boys crept in the darkness to the tavern. Huck watched. Tom felt his way into the alley. Tom was gone so long that Huck was worried. Suddenly there was a flash of light. Tom came tearing by him.

"Run!" he cried. "Run for your life!"

The boys never stopped till they reached an empty shed at the other end of town. Just as they got inside, the storm burst.

"Huck," said Tom, "it was awful! I tried two of the keys as soft as I could. They didn't work. I took hold of the door knob. Open comes the door! It wasn't locked! I went in. I took the towel off the lantern."

"What did you see, Tom?"

"Huck, I almost stepped on Injun Joe's hand!"

"No!"

"Yes! He was laying there sound asleep on the floor. His patch was on his eye. His arms was spread out."

"What did you do? Did he wake up?"

"No. He never budged. Drunk, I reckon. I just grabbed the towel and ran."

"Say, Tom, did you see that box?"

"Huck, I didn't wait to look around. I didn't see the box. I didn't see the cross. I didn't see anything but a bottle and a tin cup on the floor. I saw two barrels and lots more bottles in the room. It's just a place to get drunk in."

"But say, Tom, now's a mighty good time to get that box if Injun Joe's drunk."

"You want to try it?"

"Well, no. I reckon not."

"Let's not try until we know Joe's not in there. It's too scary. If we watch every night, we'll be sure to see him go out. Then we'll grab the box."

"That suits me. I'll watch the whole night long. You do the rest of the job."

"All right. I will. All you got to do is trot up Hooper Street and meow. If I'm asleep, throw some gravel at the window."

"Right," said Huck. "I'll sleep all day and watch all night."

"Now, Huck, the storm is over. I'll go home. It will be daylight soon. You go back and watch."

"I said I would, and I will. I'll sleep all day and watch all night."

"Now, where are you going to sleep?"

"In Ben Rogers' hayloft. He lets me and so does his father's slave, Uncle Jake. I tote water for Uncle Jake. When I ask, he gives me something to eat. He's a mighty good feller. He likes me because I don't act like I'm above him. Sometimes I sit right down and eat *with* him."

"Well, I won't need you in the daytime. I'll let you sleep. When something happens at night, come and meow."

Chapter 25

Tom had some good news Friday morning. Judge Thatcher's family came back to town. Becky teased her mother to have that picnic the next day. Mrs. Thatcher agreed. Tom didn't hear from Huck that night.

By ten o'clock next morning a crowd of young folks gathered at Judge Thatcher's house. The old steam ferryboat was rented. The happy crowd marched down Main Street with their baskets of food. Sid was sick and had to miss the fun. Mary stayed home to take care of him.

"Becky, you won't get back till late," said Mrs. Thatcher. "Maybe you'd better stay all night with some of the girls that live near the ferry landing."

"I'll stay with Susy Harper, mamma."

Tom and Becky walked along together.

"Becky, I'll tell you what we'll do. Instead of going to the Harpers, let's stop at the Widow Douglas'. She'll have ice cream! She has it every day—loads of it! She'll be awful glad to have us."

"Oh, that will be fun!"

So Tom and Becky told no one about their plans. Three miles below town, the ferryboat stopped and tied up. The crowd hurried ashore shouting and laughing. At noon they had their lunch. Then they rested a while in the shade.

"Who's ready for the cave?" somebody shouted.

Everybody was. Armed with candles, the boys and girls ran up the hill. The mouth of the cave was on the side of the hill. Its big oak door stood open. Inside was a small room, chilly as an icehouse. The main road inside the cave ran downhill. By candlelight the picnickers could see the high walls stretching sixty feet over their heads. The main road was not more than eight or ten feet wide. Every few steps other paths branched out from both sides. McDougal's Cave was a big network of crooked lanes that ran into one another. It was said that you might wander for days and never find the end of the cave. Nobody "knew" the cave. Most of the young men knew parts of it. Tom Sawyer knew as much of the cave as anybody.

By and by the boys and girls straggled back to the mouth of the cave. They were surprised to find that it was almost dark. The bell to come back had rung for a half hour. At last the ferryboat pushed off and headed back to town.

Huck was already watching when the ferryboat lights passed the landing. At ten o'clock the town lights began to wink out. At eleven the tavern lights were put out.

Suddenly Huck heard a noise. The alley door closed softly. Huck sprang to the corner of the brick store. The next moment two men brushed by him. One seemed to have something under his arm. Was it the box? Huck could not stop now to get Tom. The men would get away and never be found again. Huck followed them like a cat in his bare feet.

They moved up the river street three blocks. There they turned left up a cross street. They took the path leading up Cardiff Hill. They passed by the old Welshman's house. Huck lost them for a while in the darkness. He stopped to listen. He heard somebody clear his throat not four feet away! Huck's heart shot up to his mouth. He knew now where he was. He was about five steps from the fence stile leading into the Widow Douglas' grounds. Now there came a voice, very low. It was Joe's voice.

"Dang her, she's got company. Late as it is, she's still got the lights on."

Huck remembered that the Widow Douglas had often been kind to him. Maybe these men were going to murder her! He wanted to warn her, but he didn't see how he could. They would surely catch him. He heard a voice again.

"Well, there is company there. Better give it up."

"Give it up?" said Injun Joe. "And never have another chance to get her? As I told you before, I don't care about her money. You can have it. But her husband was hard on me. He sent me to jail as a bum. And that ain't all. He had me *horsewhipped*—horsewhipped in front of the jail. The whole town watched them *horsewhip* me. Do you understand? He died. But I'll take it out on *her*."

"Oh, don't kill her! Don't do that!"

"Kill? Who said anything about killing? I'd kill *him* if he was here, but not her. When you want to get revenge on a woman, you don't kill her. You mark her up with a knife. You cut her nose. You notch her ears like a sow!"

"By God, that's—"

"Shut up. I'll tie her to the bed. If she bleeds to death, is that my fault? My friend, you'll help me do this thing—for *my* sake. That's why you're here. I might not be able to do it alone. If you back out, I'll kill you. Do you understand that? And if I have to kill you, I'll kill her. Then nobody will know what happened."

"Well, if it's got to be done, let's get at it the quicker the better."

"Now? With company there? No. We'll wait till the lights are out. There's no hurry."

Huck stepped silently back. He took another and another step. When it was safe, he ran. He ran till he came to the Welshman's house. He banged at the door. Soon the heads of the old man and his two husky sons appeared at the windows.

"What's the noise down there? What do you want?"

"Let me in—quick! I'll tell everything."

"Who are you?"

"Huckleberry Finn! Quick, let me in!"

"That's not a name to open many doors. But let him in, lads. Let's see what's the trouble."

"Please don't ever tell I told you," cried Huck. "Please don't. I'll be killed. But the widow's been good friends to me. I *will* tell if you promise you won't ever say it was me."

"By George, he has got something to tell," said the old man. "Out with it. Nobody here will ever tell, lad."

Three minutes later the old man and his sons, well armed, went up the hill. When they came to the thick bushes, Huck stopped. He hid behind a big rock. The Welshman and his sons stepped carefully onward. There was a long silence. All of a sudden a shot rang out, and a cry of pain. Huck didn't wait. He sped down the hill as fast as his legs could carry him.

Chapter 26

As soon as the sun rose, Huck tapped softly at the old Welshman's door. A call came from a window.

"Who's there?"

"Please let me in. It's only Huck Finn."

"Welcome, Huck! Come in."

The door was quickly unlocked. The old man and his sons were soon dressed.

"I hope you're good and hungry," said the Welshman. "Breakfast will soon be ready. We hoped you'd stop here last night."

"I was awful scared," said Huck. "I ran. When the guns went off I didn't stop for three miles. I've come to find out what happened. I came early. I didn't want to see those devils even if they was dead."

"Well, you do look tired. There's a bed here for you when you've had your breakfast. No, they ain't dead, lad. We're sorry about that. We crept along on tiptoe till we got within fifteen feet of them. Just then I had to sneeze. I tried to keep it back, but I couldn't. I sang out, 'Fire, boys' and blazed away. So did the boys. But they got away. We got some men to watch the river bank. As soon as it's light we'll search the woods. I wish we knew what they looked like. That would help. I guess you couldn't see what they looked like, could you?"

"Oh, yes. I saw them in town. I followed them."

"Good! What did they look like?"

"One is the old deaf-and-dumb Spaniard that's

come to town. The other one is a mean-looking, ragged—"

"We know 'em. Saw them in the woods one day last week. Go boys. Tell the sheriff."

The Welshman's sons left.

"Oh, please don't tell *any* body it was me that told on them!" cried Huck.

"All right, if you say so, Huck. But you ought to get credit for what you did."

"Oh, no! Please don't tell!"

"They won't tell, and I won't. But why don't you want it known?"

Huck didn't have a good answer.

"How did you come to follow these fellows?"

"Well," said Huck, "last night I couldn't sleep. I come up the street about midnight. Well, just then along came these two fellows. One had something under his arm. I reckoned he'd stole it. One was smoking. The other one wanted a light. They stopped right in front of me. I see the big one was the deaf-and-dumb Spaniard. I could see his white whiskers. The other was a dusty, ragged-looking fellow."

"Could you see all that by the light of their cigars?"

"Well, uh, it *seems* like I could."

"Then they went on, and you—"

"Followed them. I wanted to see what was up. At the fence stile I heard the Spaniard say he'd spoil the widow's looks, just as I told you—"

"What? The deaf-and-dumb man said all that?"

Huck had made another mistake. He was trying to keep the old man from finding out who the so-called Spaniard might be. Pretty soon the Welshman said:

"My boy, don't be afraid of me. I wouldn't hurt

a hair of your head. I'd protect you. This Spaniard is not deaf and dumb. You've let that slip. You can't cover that up now. You know something about that Spaniard you want to keep dark. Now trust me. Tell me what it is."

Huck looked into the old man's honest eyes. Then he bent over and whispered in his ear.

"He ain't a Spaniard. It's Injun Joe."

The Welshman almost jumped out of his chair. "It's all plain enough now," he said.

He said he and his sons had taken a lantern out to the fence stile last night. They had looked for marks of blood.

"We found no blood," he said. "We did find a bundle of—"

"OF WHAT?" cried Huck.

"Of burglar's tools. That seems to make you happy. What did you expect us to find?"

Again Huck had no answer. Of course he didn't want to tell about the box of gold.

"You're pale and tired, lad," said the Welshman. "You need a rest."

Huck had found out that the thing the fellow had carried was not the box of gold. The treasure must still be in Number Two.

Just as breakfast was over, there was a knock at the door. The Welshman opened the door. In came several men and ladies. The Widow Douglas was one of the ladies. The Welshman had to tell all over what had happened. The widow thanked him for saving her life.

"Don't say a word about it, madam," said the Welshman. "You owe more to somebody else than to me. He won't let me tell his name. We wouldn't have been there but for him."

Everybody wanted to know who the hero was.

The Welshman wouldn't tell, though.

"I fell asleep reading in bed," said the Widow Douglas. "I slept through all that noise. Why didn't you come and wake me?"

"Well, those fellows wouldn't have come back. They hadn't any tools left to work with. There was no use waking you up."

More visitors came. The story had to be told for two or three hours more.

Chapter 27

There was no Sunday school during the summer. Everybody came early to church. The news was that the two robbers had not been caught. After the sermon, Mrs. Thatcher spoke to Mrs. Harper.

"Is my Becky going to sleep all day?" she said. "I guess she's tired from the picnic."

"Your Becky?"

"Yes. Didn't she stay with you last night?"

"No."

Mrs. Thatcher turned pale. She sat down on a church bench. Just then Aunt Polly passed by.

"Good morning, Mrs. Thatcher. Good morning, Mrs. Harper. I've got a boy that's missing. I reckon my Tom stayed at your house last night. I guess he's afraid to come to church. I'll settle with him."

Mrs. Thatcher grew even paler.

"He didn't stay with us," said Mrs. Harper. She began to look uneasy. Aunt Polly looked worried.

"Joe Harper, have you seen my Tom this morning?"

"No, ma'am."

"When did you see him last?"

Joe wasn't sure. The people stopped moving out of church. Whispers were passed along. Children were questioned. The young teachers were questioned. Nobody had noticed whether Tom and Becky were on the boat going home. It was dark. Nobody had thought to check. Somebody said they must still be in the cave. Mrs. Thatcher fainted. Aunt Polly started to cry.

Within five minutes the bells were ringing. The whole town was up! They forgot about the robbery attempt on Cardiff Hill. Horses were saddled. Skiffs were manned. The ferryboat was sent out. Several hundred men were quickly on the way to the cave.

The town was empty all afternoon. Women visited Aunt Polly and Mrs. Thatcher. All night the town waited for news. But when morning came, the word was, "Send more candles. Send food." Mrs. Thatcher was nearly out of her mind. So, too, was Aunt Polly.

The old Welshman came home about daylight. He was smeared with candle grease and clay. He found Huck still in bed with a bad fever. The doctors were all at the cave, so the Widow Douglas took care of Huck.

Some of the men now came back to town. The search went on, though. They were now looking in parts of the cave that nobody had seen before. Lights could be seen everywhere. People were shouting. Guns were shot in hope that they would be heard. In one place they found BECKY AND TOM on the rocky wall. They found a ribbon that had belonged to Becky. Mrs. Thatcher cried when she saw it.

Three days and nights dragged by. The town pretty well gave up hope. The sheriff found that the tavern owner was selling whiskey in his No. Two room. Huck, feeling a little better, asked if anything else had been found there.

"Yes," said the Widow Douglas.

Huck nearly fell out of bed.

"What? What was it?"

"Whiskey," said the widow. "Barrels and barrels

114

of the stuff. Lie down, child."

"Only one thing," said Huck. "Just tell me one thing. Did Tom Sawyer find it?"

The widow burst into tears.

"Hush, child!" she said. "I've told you before. You must not talk. You are very, very sick."

Huck was glad to get the news. Only whiskey had been found. So the treasure was gone—gone forever! But what was the widow crying about? A few minutes later Huck again fell asleep.

"There, he's asleep, poor boy," said the widow. "I couldn't bear to tell him about Tom Sawyer. Most everybody has given up searching."

Chapter 29

Like all the others, Tom and Becky had wandered around in the cave. They played hide-and-seek with the others. They had walked down the cave paths holding their candles high. They had a good time reading the names, dates, and addresses on the walls. Before they knew it, they were alone—far from the others. They came to a little stream of water. Behind it was a narrow stone stairway. He and Becky made a smoke mark on the wall.

"That's so we can find our way back, Becky," said Tom.

They wound their way down, deeper and deeper in the cave. They came to another spring of sparkling water. Up under the roof were bats—thousands of bats! Seeing the candle light, they came down by the hundreds. They squeaked and darted angrily at the candles. Tom grabbed Becky's hand and pulled her into another pathway. The bats chased the children a good distance. At last they got rid of the bats. They came to a big underground lake. They sat down to rest.

"It seems a long time since I heard any of the others," said Becky.

"Come to think of it, Becky, we're far below them," said Tom.

"I wonder how long we've been down here, Tom. We better start back. Can you find the way back? I'm all mixed up."

"I reckon I could. I don't like those bats,

though. If they put both our candles out, we'll be in trouble. Let's try some other way."

"I hope we won't get lost," said Becky. "That would be awful." She shivered.

All the places looked new and strange now. Tom tried to keep Becky's spirits up.

"Oh, it's all right," he would say. "This ain't the one, but we'll find it right away."

But they didn't. Becky hung onto Tom's hand, trying to hold back the tears. Tom stopped. They could hear nothing. Tom shouted.

"They might hear me, Becky," he said. He shouted again.

"Becky," he said, "I was such a fool! Such a fool! I never thought about coming back. I can't find the way. I'm all mixed up, too."

"Tom, Tom! We're lost! We're lost! We can never get out of this awful place. Oh, why did we ever leave the others?"

She sank down to the ground and burst into tears. He sat down beside her. He put his arms around her. She buried her face in his chest. He blamed himself for getting her into this awful trouble. Becky said he was no more to blame than she.

They moved on again. There was nothing else to do. By and by Tom blew out Becky's candle. Becky knew why. They might end up with no light!

At last Becky could go no farther. She sat down. Tom rested with her. Soon Becky fell asleep. At last she woke up.

"Oh, how *could* I sleep! I wish I never, never had waked! No! No, I don't Tom! Don't look like that! I won't say that again."

"Cheer up, Becky. Let's go on trying."

They came to another spring. Tom said it was

time to rest again.

"Tom, I'm so hungry."

Tom took something out of his pocket. It was a piece of cake. He had saved it from the picnic. Tom broke it in half. Becky ate her half hungrily. Tom just nibbled at his half. By and by Becky wanted to go on.

"Becky," said Tom, "we must stay here. There's water to drink. That little piece is our last candle!"

Becky burst into tears. They watched the candle melt slowly away. Then—darkness! They slept a while, then. They woke. Tom tried shouting again. The hours went by. They were both hungry. Tom had saved most of his half of the cake. He broke it in half again. There wasn't much, but they gladly ate it.

"Sh!" said Tom suddenly. "Did you hear that?"

They held their breath and listened. There was a sound like a shout. Tom yelled back. He held Becky's hand and moved forward.

"It's them!" cried Tom. "They're coming! We're all right now."

They had to go slowly. There were great holes in the paths. One false step, and they could have plunged to the bottom. The children had to feel their way back. They slept again. They awoke, hungry and hopeless. Tom thought he'd try some of the side paths. He took a kite string from his pocket. He fastened it to a rock. Then he and Becky explored the paths. When he felt a great hole ahead of them, he stopped and they went back.

He came to one of these holes and saw—a human hand holding a candle! Tom shouted. The hand was followed by a body. That body belonged to—Injun Joe! Tom was so scared, he couldn't move. Injun Joe turned and ran! He had not been able to tell it was Tom's voice. Tom didn't tell Becky what he had run into.

Again the children fell into a long sleep. Both of them were very weak now from hunger. Tom fastened his kite line again. Becky begged him to come back from time to time to speak to her. Tom kissed her gently. He took the kite string in his hand and crawled down another passage on his hands and knees.

Chapter 29

The little town of St. Petersburg was still in mourning for the lost children. They had been prayed for in church. But no good news came from the cave. Most of the searchers had given up. Mrs. Thatcher was very sick. People said it was sad to hear her call Becky's name. Aunt Polly's gray hair had turned white. The town went to bed still sorrowing on Tuesday night.

And in the middle of the night the church bells began to ring. In a few minutes the streets were swarming with half-dressed people.

"They found them! They found them!"

They beat on tin pans. They blew horns. The crowd cheered. They moved quickly to the river. Some men were pulling a wagon with Tom and Becky inside. The people cheered wildly as the children came into sight. The town was all lit up. Nobody went back to bed. It was the greatest night the little town had ever seen.

Tom told how he had explored several passageways in the cave. He had gone the full length of his kite line in one of them. He was about to turn back. He thought he saw a speck of daylight. He dropped his kite line and moved toward it. He pushed his head and shoulders through a small hole. There before him the Mississippi River was rolling by! He told how he had gone back for Becky. He pushed his way out of the hole. Then he helped Becky out. Some men came by in a skiff. Tom called to them and told his story. The men could hardly believe Tom. The children were at least five miles away from the cave opening.

The men took Tom and Becky aboard. They were rowed to a nearby house. The people there gave them supper and made them rest for a few hours. Then they brought them home.

Tom and Becky had spent three days and nights in the cave. Worn out, they had to stay in bed Wednesday and Thursday. Tom got up a while on Thursday. He was back in town on Friday and felt fine on Saturday. Becky did not leave her room till Sunday.

Tom found out about Huck's illness. He was not able to see him till Monday. The Widow Douglas kept an eye on Tom. She didn't want him to get Huck excited. Tom found out about Huck's adventure on Cardiff Hill. Injun Joe's partner had been found in the river near the ferry landing. Perhaps he was drowned when he and Joe escaped.

A week after Tom was saved, he started out to visit Huck. Judge Thatcher's house was on Tom's way, so he stopped to see Becky. The Judge and some friends got Tom talking. Somebody asked him if he wouldn't like to go to the cave again. Tom said he wouldn't mind.

"Well, there are others just like you, Tom," said Judge Thatcher. "But we've taken care of that. Nobody will get lost in that cave any more."

"Why?"

"Because I had its big door covered with iron two weeks ago. It's triple locked. I've got the only keys."

Tom turned as white as a sheet.

"What's the matter, boy? Somebody run! Fetch a glass of water!"

They threw the water in Tom's face.

"Ah, now you're all right. What was the matter with you, Tom?"

"Oh, Judge, Injun Joe is in the cave."

Chapter 30

The news about Injun Joe spread quickly. A dozen skiffs were on their way to the cave. The ferryboat, loaded with people, soon followed. Tom Sawyer was in a skiff with Judge Thatcher.

The Judge unlocked the cave door. There lay Injun Joe, stretched on the ground, dead. Joe's knife lay beside him. The blade was broken. Joe had been uselessly hacking at the great door. He had starved to death. He had caught a few bats. He had eaten them, all but their claws.

They buried Joe near the mouth of the cave. Both Tom and Huck felt a lot better. At least they no longer lived in fear of Joe's revenge.

The morning after, Tom took Huck aside for a talk. Huck had found out about Tom's adventures from the Welshman and the Widow Douglas. Tom said there was one thing they had *not* told him.

"That's what I want to talk about to you now, Huck," said Tom.

"I know what it is. You got into Number Two. You never found anything but whiskey. I always knew we'd never get that loot."

"Huck, that money wasn't ever in Number Two."

"What? Tom, are you on the track of that money again?"

"Huck, it's in the cave!"

"Say that again, Tom."

"The money's in the cave. Will you go in there with me and help get it out?"

"You bet I will."

"Huck, it'll be easy."

"What makes you think the money's in the cave?"

"Huck, you just wait till we get in there."

"All right. When do we go?"

"Right now, if you say so. Are you strong enough?"

"Is it far in the cave? I can't walk more than a mile, Tom."

"It's about five miles the way anybody else would go. There's a short cut only I know about. I'll take you right to it in a skiff."

"Let's go, Tom."

"All right. We'll want some bread and meat and our pipes. We'll need a few bags and two or three kite strings."

A little after noon the boys borrowed somebody's skiff. They paddled down to several miles past the mouth of the cave.

"See the white spot up there on the hill side, Huck? That's one of my marks. We'll go ashore here."

They landed.

"Now, Huck, from where we are you could touch the hole I got out of with Becky. Can you find it?"

Huck found nothing. Tom marched into a clump of thick bushes.

"Here you are! Look at it, Huck!"

The boys crawled into the hole. They crept to the end of the tunnel. Tom tied the kite strings to rocks. A few steps brought them to the spring. They went on, holding and unwinding the kite string. They came to a steep clay hill.

"Now I'll show you something, Huck."

He held his candle up high.

"Look at that big rock over there."

"Tom, it's a *cross!*"

"Now where's Number Two? Remember? *'Under the cross.'* That's where I saw Injun Joe!"

Tom went down the clay hill first. As he went he cut crude steps. Four passages led out of the room where the rock stood. The boys looked into three of them and found—nothing. In the fourth one they found a bed of blankets and the bones of some birds. There was no money box.

"He said *under* the cross," said Tom. "This comes nearest to being under the cross. I'll bet the money is under the rock. I'm going to dig there."

Before Tom got four inches deep he struck wood.

"Hey, Huck! Do you hear that?"

Huck started to help dig. Some loose planks came next.

"Huck! Look here!"

Sure enough, there was the box!

"Got it at last!" cried Huck. "We're rich, Tom! Let's not fool around here any longer. Let's get it out. Let me see if I can lift the box."

The box weighed about fifty pounds. It was hard to carry.

"I brought these bags to put the coins in," said Tom.

They soon had the money in the bags. They carried them out past the clump of bushes. The coast was clear, so they dumped the bags into the skiff. They had their lunch and a smoke. Then they paddled back and landed soon after dark.

"Now, Huck," said Tom, "we'll hide the money in the widow's woodshed. I'll come up in the morning. Then we'll count it and split it. You just

watch the stuff. I'll get Benny Taylor's little wagon."

Tom came back with the wagon. They put the sacks in the wagon. When the boys reached the Welshman's house, they stopped to rest. As they were about to go on, the Welshman stepped out.

"Hello, who's there?"

"Huck and Tom Sawyer."

"Good! Come along with me, boys. You're keeping everybody waiting."

The boys wanted to know why the hurry.

"Never mind. You'll see when you get to the Widow Douglas'."

The Welshman pushed the boys into Mrs. Douglas' parlor when they got there. He left the wagon outside the door.

The place was brightly lit. The Thatchers were there. The Harpers and Rogers were there, too. Aunt Polly, Sid, and Mary had come. So had the preacher and the newspaper owner. A lot more folks were there, all dressed in their best clothes.

The boys were covered with clay and candle grease.

"Tom wasn't home," said the Welshman. "I bumped into him and Huck right at my door. I just brought them along as is."

"And you did just right," said the widow. "Come with me, boys."

She took them into an empty room.

"Now wash and dress yourselves," she said. "Here are two new suits, shirts, and some socks. They belong to Huck. Mr. Jones here bought one and I the other. They'll fit both of you. Get into them. We'll wait for you. Come back downstairs when you're dressed."

Chapter 31

"Tom," said Huck, "we can get out of here if we can find a rope. The window ain't high from the ground."

"Shucks, Huck, why get out of here?"

"Well, I ain't used to that kind of a crowd. I can't stand it. I ain't going back down there, Tom."

"Oh, come on, Huck. It ain't anything. I'll be with you all the time."

Sid came into the room just then.

"Tom," he said, "Aunt Polly's been waiting for you all afternoon. Mary got your Sunday clothes ready. Say, ain't this clay and candle grease on your clothes? Where have you been?"

"Now, Sid, you just mind your own business. What's this all about?"

"The widow's having a party. It's for Jones, the Welshman, and his sons. She wants to thank them for saving her from Injun Joe. And say—I can tell you something if you want to know."

"Well, what?"

"Why, old Jones is going to spring a surprise. I overheard him tell Aunt Polly about it as a secret. I reckon it's not much of a secret *now*. Everybody knows. The widow knows, too. Jones wanted Huck to be here. Had to have Huck here for his grand secret."

"What secret, Sid?"

"About Huck tracking the robbers to the widow's house. Jones was going to make a big deal out of it. But everybody knows about it already."

Sid laughed.

"Sid, was it you that told?"

"Oh, never mind who it was. *Somebody* told."

"Sid, the only one in town mean enough to do that is you. If you'd been in Huck's place, you would have sneaked down the hill. You would never have told on the robbers. You can't do any but mean things. You can't bear to see anybody praised for doing good ones."

Tom whacked Sid's ears and helped him to the door with a swift kick.

"There!" he said. "Go and tell Aunt Polly on me if you dare. I'll give it to you good tomorrow."

A few minutes later the widow's friends were at the supper table. The children sat at little side tables. Mr. Jones made his little speech after they had eaten. He thanked the widow for honoring himself and his sons. There was another person, he said, who should be honored. That person was Huckleberry Finn. He told how brave Huck had been to follow the robbers. He told how Huck had awakened him and his sons. Nobody was very much surprised to hear the story. The widow did act surprised. She thanked Huck again and again. The others told him what a fine brave boy he was.

The widow said she wanted to give Huck a home under her roof. She would send him to school. When he grew up she said she would start him in business. That gave Tom a chance to speak.

"Huck don't need it," he said. "Huck's rich!"

Everybody thought Tom was joking, of course. There were a few polite smiles.

"Huck's got money," said Tom again. "Maybe you don't believe it. He's got lots of money. Oh, you needn't smile. I can show you. You just wait a minute."

Tom ran outside. The people looked at one another in surprise. They stared at Huck, who said nothing.

Tom came back in dragging the sacks of coins. He poured the yellow coins on the table.

"There!" he cried. "What did I tell you? Half of it belongs to Huck. The other half is mine!"

Well, that did take their breath away. Everybody stared. Nobody spoke for a minute. Then they all wanted Tom to explain. Tom's story was long, but interesting. When he had finished, the Welshman laughed.

"I thought I had a surprise for you," he said. "Tom's story is a much better one."

They counted the money. There was a little more than twelve thousand dollars. It was more than anybody there had seen at one time.

Chapter 32

Tom and Huck's treasure made a mighty stir in town. So much cash seemed unbelievable. Every haunted house for miles around was ransacked. Wherever Tom and Huck went, they were admired and stared at. The town newspaper printed stories about them.

The Widow Douglas put Huck's money in the bank to earn interest. Judge Thatcher did the same for Tom. Each boy now had an income—a dollar a day. That was for every week and half the Sundays. That was as much as the preacher was promised. Of course, he never *got* that much. In those old simple days a dollar and a quarter a week would house and feed a boy.

Judge Thatcher thought Tom Sawyer was quite a boy. He said no other boy would have got his Becky out of the cave. Becky had told him how Tom had lied to take her whipping at school. The judge said it was a noble lie. He said it was as fine as George Washington's lie about the cherry tree. Becky told Tom all about it.

Judge Thatcher hoped to see Tom become a great lawyer or a great general. He said he would see to it that Tom got to go to West Point. After that he would go to the best law school in the country.

Huck's money did not make him any happier. The widow's servants kept him clean and neat. They combed him and brushed him. They put him between clean sheets every night. He had to eat with a knife and fork. He had to use napkins, cups, and plates. He had to study his schoolbooks. He had to go to church. He had to learn to speak all over again.

Huck stuck to it for three weeks. Then one day he turned up missing. The widow hunted for him for 48 hours. Everybody helped look for him. Early the third morning Tom Sawyer went poking among the empty barrels in the tanyard. He found Huck in one of them. Huck had slept there. He had stolen some scraps for breakfast. Now he was smoking his pipe. He was dirty and uncombed. He was dressed in his old rags. Tom routed him out. He told him how much trouble he was causing.

"Come back, Huck, please," he said.

"Don't talk about it, Tom," said Huck. "I've tried it. It don't work. It ain't for me. I ain't used to it. The widder's good to me. She's friendly. But I can't stand her ways. She makes me get up the same time every morning. She makes me wash. They comb me. She won't let me sleep in the woodshed. I got to wear clothes that smother me. They're so rotten nice I can't sit down, or lay down anywheres. I got to go to church and sweat. I got to listen to those long sermons. I can't ketch a fly in there. I got to wear shoes all day Sunday. The widder eats by a bell. She goes to bed by a bell. She gets up by a bell. I just can't stand it."

"Well, everybody does that way, Huck."

"Tom, I ain't everybody. I can't *stand* it. The grub comes too easy. I don't like food like that. I got to ask to go fishing. I got to ask to go swimming. I got to ask to do anything. The widder wouldn't let me smoke. She wouldn't let me yell, or yawn, or stretch, or scratch in front of folks. And she prays all the time! I never *see* such a woman. Look here,

Tom. Being rich ain't what it's cracked up to be. It's just worry and sweat. Now these old rags suit me. This old barrel suits me. I wouldn't ever have got into this trouble if it hadn't been for that money. Now you take my share. You go and beg me off with the widder."

"Oh, Huck, you know I can't do that. It ain't fair. Besides, if you'll try this thing a while longer, you'll come to like it."

"Like it! Yes, the way I'd like a hot stove if I'd sit on it long enough. No, Tom, I won't be rich. I won't live in those stuffy houses. I like the woods and the river. Blame it all, just after we get Injun Joe's guns and a cave, this foolishness has to spoil it all."

"Look here, Huck. Being rich ain't going to keep me from being a robber."

"No! You mean it, Tom?"

"Sure I mean it. But Huck, we can't let you in the robber gang if you ain't a respected person."

"Can't you let me in, Tom? You let me in the pirate gang."

"Yes, but that was different, Huck. A robber is more high-toned than a pirate. In most countries they're as high as dukes."

"Now, Tom, ain't you always been friendly to me? You wouldn't shut me out, would you?"

"Huck, I wouldn't want to. I *don't* want to. But what would people say? They'd say, 'Tom Sawyer's Gang? It's got slobs in it.' They'd mean you, Huck. You wouldn't like that. I wouldn't either."

Huck thought it over a long time.

"Well," he said, "I'll go back to the widder for a month. I'll see if I can get to stand it if you'll let me belong to the gang, Tom."

"All right, Huck. I'll ask the widow to let up on

you a little."

"Will you, Tom? If she'll let up a little, I'll smoke in private. When you going to start the gang and turn robbers?"

"Oh, right off. We'll get the boys together and have the swearing in tonight."

"What's the swearing in, Tom?"

"You swear to stand by one another. You swear to kill anybody and his family if he hurts one of the gang."

"That's good, Tom!"

"You got to swear in a haunted house at midnight. You got to swear on a coffin and sign your name in blood."

"Now that's something like it! That's better than being a pirate. I'll stick with the widder, Tom. I reckon she'll be proud she gave me a chance to be a robber."